THE
TROUBADOURS

BY

REV. H. J. CHAYTOR, M. A.

KENNIKAT PRESS
Port Washington, N. Y./London

THE TROUBADOURS

First published in 1912
Reissued in 1970 by Kennikat Press
Library of Congress Catalog Card No: 74-102836
SBN 8046-0751-6

Manufactured by Taylor Publishing Company   Dallas, Texas

PREFACE

THIS book, it is hoped, may serve as an introduction to the literature of the Troubadours for readers who have no detailed or scientific knowledge of the subject. I have, therefore, chosen for treatment the Troubadours who are most famous or who display characteristics useful for the purpose of this book. Students who desire to pursue the subject will find further help in the works mentioned in the bibliography. The latter does not profess to be exhaustive, but I hope nothing of real importance has been omitted.

H. J. CHAYTOR.

THE COLLEGE,
PLYMOUTH, *March* 1912.

CONTENTS

THE TROUBADOURS

CHAPTER I

INTRODUCTORY

FEW literatures have exerted so profound an influence upon the literary history of other peoples as the poetry of the troubadours. Attaining the highest point of technical perfection in the last half of the twelfth and the early years of the thirteenth century, Provençal poetry was already popular in Italy and Spain when the Albigeois crusade devastated the south of France and scattered the troubadours abroad or forced them to seek other means of livelihood. The earliest lyric poetry of Italy is Provençal in all but language; almost as much may be said of Portugal and Galicia; Catalonian troubadours continued to write in Provençal until the fourteenth century. The lyric poetry of the "trouvères" in Northern France was deeply influenced both in form and spirit by troubadour poetry, and traces of this influence are perceptible even in early middle-English lyrics. Finally, the German minnesingers knew and appreciated troubadour lyrics, and imitations or even translations of Provençal poems may be found in Heinrich von Morungen, Friedrich von Hausen, and many others. Hence the poetry of the troubadours is a subject of first-rate importance to the student of comparative literature.

The northern limit of the Provençal language formed a line starting from the Pointe de Grave at the mouth of the Gironde, passing through Lesparre, Bordeaux, Libourne, Périgueux, rising northward to Nontron, la Rochefoucauld, Confolens, Bellac, then turning eastward to Guéret and Montluçon ; it then went south-east to Clermont-Ferrand, Boën, Saint Georges, Saint Sauveur near Annonay. The Dauphiné above Grenoble, most of the Franche-Comté, French Switzerland and Savoy, are regarded as a separate linguistic group known as Franco-Provençal, for the reason that the dialects of that district display characteristics common to both French and Provençal.[1] On the south-west, Catalonia, Valencia and the Balearic Isles must also be included in the Provençal region. As concerns the Northern limit, it must not be regarded as a definite line of demarcation between the langue d'oil or the Northern French dialects and the langue d'oc or Provençal. The boundary is, of course, determined by noting the points at which certain linguistic features peculiar to Provençal cease and are replaced by the characteristics of Northern French. Such a characteristic, for instance, is the Latin tonic *a* before a single consonant, and not preceded by a palatal consonant, which remains in Provençal but becomes *e* in French ; Latin cant*a*re becomes chant*a*r in Provençal but chant*e*r in French. But north and south of the boundary thus determined there was, in the absence of any great mountain range or definite geographical line of demarcation, an indeterminate zone, in which one dialect probably shaded off by easy gradations into the other.

Within the region thus described as Provençal, several separate dialects existed, as at the present day. Apart from the Franco-Provençal on the north-east, which we have excluded, there was Gascon in the south-west and the modern *départements* of the Basses and Hautes Pyrénées ; Catalonian, the dialect of Roussillon, which was brought into Spain in the seventh century and still survives in Catalonia, Valencia and the Balearic Islands. The rest of the country may be subdivided by a line to the north of which *c* before *a* becomes *ch* as in French, cant*a*re producing chant*a*r, while southwards we find *c* (*k*) remaining. The Southern dialects are those of Languedoc and Provence ; north of the line were the Limousin and Auvergne dialects. At the present day these dialects have diverged very widely. In the early middle ages the difference between them was by no means so great. Moreover, a literary language grew up by degrees, owing to the wide circulation of poems and the necessity of using a dialect which could be universally intelligible. It was the Limousin dialect which became, so to speak, the backbone of this literary language, now generally known as Provençal, just as the Tuscan became predominant for literary purposes among the Italian dialects. It was in Limousin that the earliest troubadour lyrics known to us were composed, and this district with the adjacent Poitou and Saintonge may therefore be reasonably regarded as the birthplace of Provençal lyric poetry.

Hence the term " Provençal " is not entirely appropriate to describe the literary language of the troubadours, as it may also be restricted to denote the dialects spoken in the " Provincia." This difficulty was felt at an early date. The first troubadours spoke of their language as *roman* or *lingua romana*, a term equally applicable to any other romance language. *Lemosin* was also used, which was too restricted a term, and was also appropriated by the Catalonians to denote their own dialect. A third term in use was the *lingua d'oc*, which has the authority of Dante [2] and was used by some of the later troubadours ; however, the term " Provençal " has been generally accepted, and must henceforward be understood to denote the literary language common to the south of France and not the dialect of Provence properly so-called.

For obvious reasons Southern France during the early middle ages had far outstripped the Northern provinces in art, learning, and the refinements of civilisation. Roman culture had made its way into Southern Gaul at an early date and had been readily accepted by the inhabitants, while Marseilles and Narbonne had also known something of Greek civilisation. Bordeaux, Toulouse, Arles, Lyons and other towns were flourishing and brilliant centres of civilisation at a time when Northern France was struggling with foreign invaders. It was in Southern Gaul, again, that Christianity first obtained a footing; here the barbarian invasions of the fifth and sixth centuries proved less destructive to civilisation than in Northern France, and the Visigoths seem to have been more amenable to the influences of culture than the Northern Franks. Thus the towns of Southern Gaul apparently remained centres in which artistic and literary traditions were preserved more or less successfully until the revival of classical studies during the age of Charlemagne. The climate, again, of Southern France is milder and warmer than that of the North, and these influences produced a difference which may almost be termed racial. It is a difference visible even to-day and is well expressed by the chronicler Raoul de Caen, who speaks of the Provençal Crusaders, saying that the French were prouder in bearing and more war-like in action than the Provençals, who especially contrasted with them by their skill in procuring food in times of famine : " inde est, quod adhuc puerorum decantat nænia, Franci ad bella, Provinciales ad victualia." [3] Only a century and a half later than Charlemagne appeared the first poetical productions in Provençal which are known to us, a fragment of a commentary upon the De Consolatione of Boethius [4] and a poem upon St Foy of Agen. The first troubadour, William, Count of Poitiers, belongs to the close of the eleventh century.

Though the Count of Poitiers is the first troubadour known to us, the relatively high excellence of his technique, as regards stanza construction and rime, and the capacity of his language for expressing lofty and refined ideas in poetical form (in spite of his occasional lapses into coarseness), entirely preclude the supposition that he was the first troubadour in point of time. The artistic conventions apparent in his poetry and his obviously careful respect for fixed rules oblige us to regard his poetry as the outcome of a considerable stage of previous development. At what point this development began and what influences stimulated its progress are questions which still remain in dispute. Three theories have been proposed. It is, in the first place, obviously tempting to explain the origin of Provençal poetry as being a continuation of Latin poetry in its decadence. When the Romans settled in Gaul they brought with them their amusements as well as their laws and institutions. Their *scurræ, thymelici* and *joculatores*, the tumblers, clowns and mountebanks, who amused the common people by day and the nobles after their banquets by night and travelled from town to town in pursuit of their livelihood, were accustomed to accompany their performances by some sort of rude song and music. In the uncivilised North they remained buffoons ; but in the South, where the greater refinement of life demanded more artistic performance, the musical part of their entertainment became predominant and the *joculator* became the *joglar* (Northern French, *jongleur*), a wandering musician and eventually a troubadour, a composer of his own poems. These latter were no longer the gross and coarse songs of the earlier mountebank age, which Alcuin characterised as *turpissima* and *vanissima*, but the grave and artificially wrought stanzas of the troubadour *chanso*.

Secondly, it has been felt that some explanation is required to account for the extreme complexity and artificiality of troubadour poetry in its most highly developed stage. Some nine hundred different forms of stanza construction are to be found in the body of troubadour poetry,[5] and few, if any schools of lyric poetry in the world, can show a higher degree of technical perfection in point of metrical diversity, complex stanza construction and accuracy in the use of rime. This result has been ascribed to Arabic influence during the eighth century ; but no sufficient proof has ever been produced that the complexities of Arabic and Provençal poetry have sufficient in common to make this hypothesis anything more than an ingenious conjecture.

One important fact stands in contradiction to these theories. All indications go to prove that the origin of troubadour poetry can be definitely localised in a particular part of Southern France. We have seen that the Limousin dialect became the basis of the literary language, and that the first troubadour known to us belonged to Poitou. It is also apparent that in the Poitou district, upon the border line of the French and Provençal languages, popular songs existed and were current among the country people ; these were songs in honour of spring, pastorals or dialogues between a knight and a shepherdess (our " Where are you going, my pretty maid ? " is of the same type), *albas* or dawn songs which represent a friend as watching near the meeting-place of a lover and his lady and giving him due warning of the approach of dawn or of any other danger ; there are also *ballatas* or dance songs of an obviously popular type.[6] Whatever influence may have been exercised by the Latin poetry of the decadence or by Arab poetry, it is in these popular and native productions that we must look for the origins of the troubadour lyrics. This popular poetry with its simple themes and homely treatment of them is to be found in many countries, and diversity of race is often no bar to strange coincidence in the matter of this poetry. It is thus useless to attempt to fix any date for the beginnings of troubadour poetry ; its primitive form doubtless existed as soon as the language was sufficiently advanced to become a medium of poetical expression.

Some of these popular themes were retained by the troubadours, the *alba* and *pastorela* for instance, and were often treated by them in a direct and simple manner. The Gascon troubadour Cercamon is said to have composed pastorals in " the old style." But in general, between troubadour poetry and the popular poetry of folk-lore, a great gulf is fixed, the gulf of artificiality. The very name " troubadour " points to this characteristic. *Trobador* is the oblique case of the nominative *trobaire*, a substantive from the verb *trobar*, in modern French *trouver*. The Northern French *trouvère* is a nominative form, and *trouveor* should more properly correspond with *trobador*. The accusative form, which should have persisted, was superseded by the nominative *trouvère*, which grammarians brought into fashion at the end of the eighteenth century. The verb *trobar* is said to be derived from the low Latin *tropus* (τρόπος), an air or melody : hence the primitive meaning of *trobador* is the " composer " or " inventor," in the first instance, of new melodies. As such, he differs from the *vates*, the inspired bard of the Romans and the ποιητής, poeta, the creative poet of the Greeks, the " maker " of Germanic literature. Skilful variation upon a given theme, rather than inspired or creative power, is generally characteristic of the troubadour.

Thus, whatever may have been the origin of troubadour poetry, it appears at the outset of the twelfth century as a poetry essentially aristocratic, intended for nobles and for courts, appealing but rarely to the middle classes and to the common people not at all. The environment which enabled this poetry to exist was provided by the feudal society of Southern France. Kings, princes and nobles themselves pursued the art and also became the patrons of troubadours who had risen from the lower classes. Occasionally troubadours existed with sufficient resources of their own to remain independent ; Folquet of Marseilles seems to have been a merchant of wealth, above the necessity of seeking patronage. But troubadours such as Bernart de Ventadour, the son of the stoker in the castle of Ventadour, Perdigon the son of a fisherman, and many others of like origin depended for their livelihood and advancement upon the favour of patrons. Thus the troubadour ranks included all sorts and conditions of men ; monks and church-men were to be found among them, such as the monk of Montaudon and Peire Cardenal, though the Church looked somewhat askance upon the profession. Women are also numbered among the troubadours ; Beatrice, the Countess of Die, is the most famous of these.

A famous troubadour usually circulated his poems by the mouth of a *joglar* (Northern French, *jongleur*), who recited them at different courts and was often sent long distances by his master for this purpose. A joglar of originality might rise to the position of a troubadour, and a troubadour who fell upon evil days might sink to the profession of joglar. Hence there was naturally some confusion between the troubadour and the joglar, and poets sometimes combined the two functions. In course of time the joglar was regarded with some contempt, and like his forbear, the Roman joculator, was classed with the jugglers, acrobats, animal tamers and clowns who amused the nobles after their feasts. Nor, under certain conditions, was the troubadour's

position one of dignity ; when he was dependent
upon his patron's bounty, he would stoop to threats
or to adulation in order to obtain the horse or the
garments or the money of his desire ; such largesse,
in fact, came to be denoted by a special term,
messio.   Jealousy   between   rival   troubadours,
accusations of slander in their poems and quarrels
with   their   patrons   were   of   constant   occurrence.
These naturally affected the joglars in their service,
who received a share of any gifts that the troubadour
might obtain.

The troubadours who were established more or
less permanently as court poets under a patron lord
were few ; a wandering life and a desire for change
of scene is characteristic of the class.   They travelled
far and wide, not only to France, Spain and Italy,
but to the Balkan peninsula, Hungary, Cyprus,
Malta and England ; Elias Cairel is said to have
visited most of the then known world, and the
biographer of Albertet Calha relates, as an unusual
fact, that this troubadour never left his native
district.   Not only love, but all social and political
questions of the age attracted their attention.
They satirised political and religious opponents,
preached crusades, sang funeral laments upon the
death of famous patrons, and the support of their
poetical powers was often in demand by princes
and nobles involved in a struggle.   Noteworthy

also is the fact that a considerable number retired to some monastery or religious house to end their days (*se rendet*, was the technical phrase). So Bertran of Born, Bernart of Ventadour, Peire Rogier, Cadenet and many others retired from the disappointments of the world to end their days in peace ; Folquet of Marseilles, who similarly entered the Cistercian order, became abbot of his monastery of Torondet, Bishop of Toulouse, a leader of the Albigeois crusade and a founder of the Inquisition.

CHAPTER II

THE THEORY OF COURTLY LOVE

TROUBADOUR poetry dealt with war, politics, personal satire and other subjects : but the theme which is predominant and in which real originality was shown, is love. The troubadours were the first lyric poets in mediæval Europe to deal exhaustively with this subject, and as their attitude was imitated with certain modifications by French, Italian, Portuguese and German poets, the nature of its treatment is a matter of considerable importance.

Of the many ladies whose praises were sung or whose favours were desired by troubadours, the majority were married. Troubadours who made their songs to a maiden, as did Gui d'Ussel or Gausbert de Puegsibot, are quite exceptional. Love in troubadour poetry was essentially a conventional relationship, and marriage was not its object. This conventional character was derived from the fact that troubadour love was constituted upon the analogy of feudal relationship. If chivalry was the outcome of the Germanic theory of knighthood as modified by the influence of Christianity, it may be said that troubadour love is the outcome of the same theory under the influence of mariolatry. In the eleventh century the worship of the Virgin Mary became widely popular ; the reverence bestowed upon the Virgin was extended to the female sex in general, and as a vassal owed obedience to his feudal overlord, so did he owe service and devotion to his lady. Moreover, under the feudal system, the lady might often be called upon to represent her husband's suzerainty to his vassals, when she was left in charge of affairs during his absence in time of war. Unmarried women were inconspicuous figures in the society of the age.

Thus there was a service of love as there was a service of vassalage, and the lover stood to his lady in a position analogous to that of the vassal to his overlord. He attained this position only by stages ; " there are four stages in love : the first is that of aspirant (*fegnedor*), the second that of suppliant (*precador*), the third that of recognised suitor (*entendedor*) and the fourth that of accepted lover (*drut*)." The lover was formally installed as such by the lady, took an oath of fidelity to her and received a kiss to seal it, a ring or some other personal possession. For practical purposes the contract merely implied that the lady was prepared to receive the troubadour's homage in poetry and to be the subject of his song. As secrecy was a duty incumbent upon the troubadour, he usually referred to the lady by a pseudonym (*senhal*) ; naturally, the lady's reputation was increased if her attraction for a famous troubadour was known, and the *senhal* was no doubt an open secret at times. How far or how often the bounds of his formal and conventional relationship were transgressed is impossible to say ; " en somme, assez immoral " is the judgment of Gaston Paris upon the society of the age, and is confirmed by expressions of desire occurring from time to time in various troubadours, which cannot be interpreted as the outcome of a merely conventional or " platonic " devotion. In the troubadour biographies the substratum of historical truth is so overlaid by fiction, that little reliable evidence upon the point can be drawn from this source.

However, transgression was probably exceptional. The idea of troubadour love was intellectual rather than emotional ; love was an art, restricted, like poetry, by formal rules ; the terms " love " and "poetry" were identified, and the fourteenth century treatise which summarises the principles of grammar and metre bore the title *Leys d'Amors*, the Laws of Love. The pathology of the emotion was studied ; it was treated from a psychological standpoint and a technical vocabulary came into use, for which it is often impossible to find English equivalents.

The first effect of love is to produce a mental exaltation, a desire to live a life worthy of the beloved
lady and redounding to her praise, an inspiring
stimulus known as *joi* or *joi d'amor* (*amor* in
Provençal is usually feminine).[7] Other virtues are
produced by the influence of this affection : the
lover must have *valor*, that is, he must be worthy
of his lady ; this worth implies the possession of
cortesia, pleasure in the pleasure of another and the
desire to please ; this quality is acquired by the
observance of *mesura*, wisdom and self-restraint
in word and deed.

The poetry which expresses such a state of mind
is usually idealised and pictures the relationship
rather as it might have been than as it was. The
troubadour who knew his business would begin
with praises of his beloved ; she is physically and
morally perfect, her beauty illuminates the night,
her presence heals the sick, cheers the sad, makes
the boor courteous and so forth. For her the
singer's love and devotion is infinite : separation
from her would be worse than death ; her death
would leave the world cheerless, and to her he owes
any thoughts of good or beauty that he may have.
It is only because he loves her that he can sing.
Hence he would rather suffer any pain or punish-
ment at her hands than receive the highest favours
from another. The effects of this love are obvious

B

in his person. His voice quavers with supreme delight or breaks in dark despair; he sighs and weeps and wakes at night to think of the one subject of contemplation. Waves of heat and cold pass over him, and even when he prays, her image is before his eyes. This passion has transformed his nature: he is a better and stronger man than ever before, ready to forgive his enemies and to undergo any physical privations; winter is to him as the cheerful spring, ice and snow as soft lawns and flowery meads. Yet, if unrequited, his passion may destroy him; he loses his self-control, does not hear when he is addressed, cannot eat or sleep, grows thin and feeble, and is sinking slowly to an early tomb. Even so, he does not regret his love, though it lead to suffering and death; his passion grows ever stronger, for it is ever supported by hope. But if his hopes are realised, he will owe everything to the gracious favour of his lady, for his own merits can avail nothing. Sometimes he is not prepared for such complete self-renunciation; he reproaches his lady for her coldness, complains that she has led him on by a show of kindness, has deceived him and will be the cause of his death; or his patience is at an end, he will live in spite of her and try his fortune elsewhere.[8]

Such, in very general terms, is the course that might be followed in developing a well-worn theme, on which many variations are possible. The most common form of introduction is a reference to the spring or winter, and to the influence of the seasons upon the poet's frame of mind or the desire of the lady or of his patron for a song. In song the poet seeks consolation for his miseries or hopes to increase the renown of his lady. As will be seen in the following chapter, manner was even more important than matter in troubadour lyrics, and commonplaces were revivified by intricate rime-schemes and stanza construction accompanied by new melodies. The conventional nature of the whole business may be partly attested by the fact that no undoubted instance of death or suicide for love has been handed down to us.

Reference should here be made to a legendary institution which seems to have gripped the imagination of almost every tourist who writes a book of travels in Southern France, the so-called *Courts of Love.*[9] In modern times the famous Provençal scholar, Raynouard, attempted to demonstrate the existence of these institutions, relying upon the evidence of the *Art d'Aimer* by André le Chapelain, a work written in the thirteenth century and upon the statements of Nostradamus (*Vies des plus célèbres et anciens poètes provençaux*, Lyons 1575). The latter writer, the younger brother of the famous prophet, was obviously well acquainted with Provençal literature and had access to sources of information which are now lost to us. But instead of attempting to write history, he embellished the lives of the troubadours by drawing upon his own extremely fertile imagination when the actual facts seemed too dull or prosaic to arouse interest. He professed to have derived his information from a manuscript left by a learned monk, the *Moine des Iles d'Or*, of the monastery of St Honorat in the Ile de Lerins. The late M. Camille Chabaneau has shown that the story is a pure fiction, and that the monk's pretended name was an anagram upon the name of a friend of Nostradamus.[10] Hence it is almost impossible to separate the truth from the fiction in this book and any statements made by Nostradamus must be received with the utmost caution. André le Chapelain seems to have had no intention to deceive, but his knowledge of Provençal society was entirely second-hand, and his statements concerning the Courts of Love are no more worthy of credence than those of Nostradamus. According to these two unreliable authorities, courts for the decision of lovers' perplexities existed in Gascony, Provence, Avignon and elsewhere ; the seat of justice was held by some famous lady, and the courts decided such questions as whether a lover could love two ladies at the same time, whether lovers or married couples were the more affectionate, whether love was compatible with avarice, and the like.

A special poetical form which was popular among the troubadours may have given rise to the legend. This was the *tenso*,[11] in which one troubadour propounded a problem of love in an opening stanza and his opponent or interlocutor gave his view in a second stanza, which preserved the metre and rime-scheme of the first. The propounder then replied, and if, as generally, neither would give way, a proposal was made to send the problem to a troubadour-patron or to a lady for settlement, a proposal which came to be a regular formula for concluding the contest. Raynouard quotes the conclusion of a *tenso* given by Nostradamus in which one of the interlocutors says, "I shall overcome you if the court is loyal : I will send the *tenso* to Pierrefeu, where the fair lady holds her court of instruction." The "court" here in question was a social and not a judicial court. Had any such institution as a judicial "court of love" ever been an integral part of Provençal custom, it is scarcely conceivable that we should be informed of its existence only by a few vague and scattered allusions in the large body of Provençal literature. For these reasons the theory that such an institution existed has been generally rejected by all scholars of repute.

CHAPTER III

PROVENÇAL literature contains examples of almost every poetical *genre*. Epic poetry is represented by Girart of Roussillon,[12] a story of long struggles between Charles Martel and one of his barons, by the Roman de Jaufre, the adventures of a knight of the Round Table, by Flamenca, a love story which provides an admirable picture of the manners and customs of the time, and by other fragments and *novelas* or shorter stories in the same style. Didactic poetry includes historical works such as the poem of the Albigeois crusade, ethical or moralising *ensenhamens* and religious poetry. But the dominating element in Provençal literature is lyrical, and during the short classical age of this literature lyric poetry was supreme. Nearly five hundred different troubadours are known to us at least by name and almost a thousand different stanza forms have been enumerated. While examples of the fine careless rapture of inspiration are by no means wanting, artificiality reigns supreme in the majority of cases. Questions of technique receive the most sedulous attention, and the principles of stanza construction, rime correspondence and rime distribution as evolved by the troubadours, exerted so wide an influence upon other European literature that they deserve a chapter to themselves.

There was no formal school for poetical training during the best period of Provençal lyric. When, for instance, Giraut de Bornelh is said to have gone to " school " during the winter seasons, nothing more is meant than the pursuit of the trivium and quadrivium, the seven arts, which formed the usual subjects of instruction. A troubadour learned the principles of his art from other poets who were well acquainted with the conventions that had been formulated in course of time, conventions which were collected and systematised in such treatises as the Leys d'Amors during the period of the decadence.

The love song or *chanso* was composed of five, six or seven stanzas (*coblas*) with one or two *tornadas* or *envois*. The stanza varied in length from two to forty-two lines, though these limits are, of course, exceptional. An earlier form of the *chanso* was known as the *vers*; it seems to have been in closer relation to the popular poetry than the more artificial *chanso*, and to have had shorter stanzas and lines; but the distinction is not clear. As all poems were intended to be sung, the poet was also a composer; the biography of Jaufre Rudel, for instance, says that this troubadour "made many poems with good tunes but poor words." The tune known as *son* (diminutive sonnet) was as much the property of a troubadour as his poem, for it implied and would only suit a special form of stanza ; hence if another poet borrowed it, acknowledgment was generally made. Dante, in his *De Vulgari Eloquentia*, informs us concerning the structure of this musical setting : it might be continuous without repetition or division ; or it might be in two parts, one repeating the other, in which case the stanza was also divided into two parts, the division being termed by Dante the *diesis* or *volta* ; of these two parts one might be subdivided into two or even more parts, which parts, in the stanza, corresponded both in rimes and in the arrangement of the lines. If the first part of the stanza was thus divisible, the parts were called *pedes*, and the musical theme or *oda* of the first *pes* was repeated for the second ; the rest of the stanza was known as the *syrma* or *coda*, and had a musical theme of its own. Again the first part of the stanza might be indivisible, when it was called the *frons*, the divided parts of the second half being the *versus* ; in this case the *frons* had its own musical theme, as did the first *versus*, the theme of the first *versus* being repeated for the second. Or, lastly, a stanza might consist of *pedes* and *versus*, one theme being used for the first *pes* and repeated for the second and similarly with the *versus*. Thus the general principle upon which the stanza was constructed was that of tripartition in the following three forms :—

I		II	
1st line 2nd ,, 3rd ,, etc.	} Pes	1st line 2nd ,, 3rd ,, etc.	} Frons
		Diesis or Volta	
1st line 2nd ,, 3rd ,, etc.	} Pes	1st line 2nd ,, 3rd ,, etc.	} Versus
Diesis or Volta			
1st line 2nd ,, 3rd ,, etc.	} Syrma or Coda	1st line 2nd ,, 3rd ,, etc.	} Versus

III

1st line 2nd ,, 3rd ,, etc.	} Pes	1st line 2nd ,, 3rd ,, etc.	} Versus
1st line 2nd ,, 3rd ,, etc.	} Pes	1st line 2nd ,, 3rd ,, etc.	} Versus
Diesis or Volta.			

These forms were rather typical than stringently binding as Dante himself notes (*De Vulg. El.*, ii. 11) ;

many variations were possible. The first seems to have been the most popular type. The poem might also conclude with a half stanza or *tornada* (French *envoi*). Here, as in the last couplet of the Arabic *gazul*, were placed the personal allusions, and when these were unintelligible to the audience the *joglar* usually explained the poem before singing it ; the explanations, which in some cases remain prefixed to the poem, were known as the *razos*.

Troubadour poems were composed for singing, not for recitation, and the music of a poem was an element of no less importance than the words. Troubadours are described as composing " good " tunes and " poor " words, or vice versa ; the tune was a piece of literary property, and, as we have said, if a troubadour borrowed a tune he was expected to acknowledge its origin. Consequently music and words were regarded as forming a unity, and the structure of the one should be a guide to the structure of the other. Troubadour music is a subject still beset with difficulties [13] : we possess 244 tunes written in Gregorian notation, and as in certain cases the same poem appears in different MSS. with the tune in substantial agreement in each one, we may reasonably assume that we have an authentic record, as far as this could be expressed in Gregorian notation. The chief difference between Troubadour and Gregorian music lies in the fact that the former was syllabic in character ; in other words, one note was not held over several syllables, though several notes might be sung upon one syllable. The system of musical time in the age of the troubadours was based upon the so-called " modes," rhythmical formulæ combining short and long notes in various sequences. Three of these concern us here. The first mode consists of a long followed by a short note, the long being equivalent to two short, or in $\frac{3}{4}$ time ♩♩. The second mode is the reverse of the first ♩♩. The third mode in modern $\frac{6}{8}$ time appears as ♩♪♪. The principle of sub-division is thus ternary ; " common " time or $\frac{2}{4}$ time is a later modification. So much being admitted, the problem of transposing a tune written in Gregorian notation without bars, time signature, marks of expression or other modern devices is obviously a difficult matter. J. Beck, who has written most recently upon the subject, formulates the following rules ; the musical accent falls upon the tonic syllables of the words ; should the accent fall upon an atonic syllable, the duration of the note to which the tonic syllable is sung may be increased, to avoid the apparent discordance between the musical accent and the tonic syllable. The musical accent must fall upon the rime and the rhythm adopted at the outset will persist throughout the poem.

Hence a study of the words will give the key to the interpretation of the tune. If, for instance, the poem shows accented followed by unaccented syllables or trochees as the prevalent foot, the first " mode " is indicated as providing the principle to be followed in transposing the Gregorian to modern notation. When these conditions are reversed the iambic foot will prevail and the melody will be in the second mode. It is not possible here to treat this complicated question in full detail for which reference must be made to the works of J. Beck. But it is clear that the system above outlined is an improvement upon that proposed by such earlier students of the subject as Riemann, who assumed that each syllable was sung to a note or group of notes of equal time value. There is no evidence that such a rhythm was ever employed in the middle ages, and the fact that words and music were inseparable in Provençal lyrics shows that to infer the nature of the musical rhythm from the rhythm of the words is a perfectly legitimate method of inquiry.

A further question arises : how far do the tunes correspond with the structure of the stanza as given by Dante ? In some cases both tune and stanza correspond in symmetrical form ; but in others we find stanzas which may be divided according to rule conjoined with tunes which present no melodic repetition of any kind ; similarly, tunes which may be divided into pedes and coda are written upon stanzas which have no relation to that form. On the whole, it seems that the number of tunes known to us are too few, in comparison with the large body of lyric poetry existing, to permit any generalisation upon the question. The singer accompanied himself upon a stringed instrument (*viula*) or was accompanied by other performers ; various forms of wind instruments were also in use. Apparently the accompaniment was in unison with the singer ; part writing or contrapuntal music was unknown at the troubadour period.

As has been said, the stanza (*cobla*) might vary in length. No poetical literature has made more use of rime than Provençal lyric poetry. There were three typical methods of rime disposition : firstly, the rimes might all find their answer within the stanza, which was thus a self-contained whole ; secondly, the rimes might find their answer within the stanza and be again repeated in the same order in all following stanzas ; and thirdly, the rimes might find no answer within the stanza, but be repeated in following stanzas. In this case the rimes were known as *dissolutas*, and the stanza as

a *cobla estrampa*. This last arrangement tended
to make the poem a more organic whole than was
possible in the first two cases ; in these, stanzas
might be omitted without necessarily impairing the
general effect, but, when *coblas estrampas* were
employed, the ear of the auditor, attentive for the
answering rimes, would not be satisfied before the
conclusion of the second stanza. A further step
towards the provision of closer unity between the
separate stanzas was the *chanso redonda*, which was
composed of *coblas estrampas*, the rime order of
the second stanza being an inversion of the rime
order of the first ; the tendency reaches its highest
point in the *sestina*, which retained the characteristic of the *chanso redonda*, namely, that the last
rime of one stanza should correspond with the
first rime of the following stanza, but with the
additional improvement that every rime staited
a stanza in turn, whereas, in the *chanso redonda*
the same rime continually recurred at the beginning
of every other stanza.

Reference has already been made to the *chanso*.
A poetical form of much importance was the *sirventes*, which outwardly was indistinguishable from
the *chanso*. The meaning of the term is unknown ;
some say that it originally implied a poem composed by " servants," poets in the service of an
overlord ; others, that it was a poem composed

to the tune of a *chanso* which it thus imitated in a
" servile " manner. From the *chanso* the *sirventes*
is distinguished by its subject matter ; it was the
vehicle for satire, moral reproof or political lampooning. The troubadours were often keenly
interested in the political events of their time ;
they filled, to some extent, the place of the modern
journalist and were naturally the partisans of the
overlord in whose service or pay they happened
to be. They were ready to foment a war, to lampoon
a stingy patron, to ridicule one another, to abuse
the morality of the age as circumstances might
dictate. The crusade *sirventes* [14] are important in
this connection, and there were often eloquent
exhortations to the leaders of Christianity to come
to the rescue of Palestine and the Holy Sepulchre.
Under this heading also falls the *planh*, a funeral
song lamenting the death of a patron, and here
again, beneath the mask of conventionality, real
emotion is often apparent, as in the famous lament
upon Richard Cœur de Lion composed by Gaucelm
Faidit.

Reference has been already made to the *tenso*,
one of the most characteristic of Provençal lyric
forms. The name (Lat. *tentionem*) implies a con-
tention or strife, which was conducted in the form
of a dialogue and possibly owed its origin to the
custom in early vogue among many different peoples

of holding poetical tournaments, in which one poet challenged another by uttering a poetical phrase to which the opponent replied in similar metrical form. Such, at any rate, is the form of the *tenso* ; a poet propounds a theme in the first stanza and his interlocutor replies in a stanza of identical metrical form ; the dispute usually continues for some half dozen stanzas. One class of tenso was obviously fictitious, as the dialogue is carried on with animals or even lifeless objects, such as a lady's cloak, and it is possible that some at least of the discussions ostensibly conducted between two poets may have emanated from the brain of one sole author. Sometimes three or four interlocutors take part ; the subject of discussion was then known as a *joc partit*, a divided game, or *partimen*, a title eventually transferred to the poem itself. The most varied questions were discussed in the *tenso*, but casuistical problems concerning love are the most frequent : Is the death or the treachery of a loved one easier to bear ? Is a lover's feeling for his lady stronger before she has accepted him or afterwards ? Is a bad noble or a poor but upright man more worthy to find favour ? The discussion of such questions provided an opportunity of displaying both poetical dexterity and also dialectical acumen. But rarely did either of the disputants declare himself convinced or vanquished by his

opponents' arguments the question was left un-
decided or was referred by agreement to an
arbitrator.

A poetical form which preserves some trace of
its popular origin is the *pastorela* [15] or pastoral
which takes its name from the fact that the heroine
of the piece was always a shepherdess. The conventional opening is a description by a knight of
his meeting with a shepherdess, " the other day "
(*l'autrier*, the word with which the poem usually
begins). A dialogue then follows between the
knight and the shepherdess, in which the former
sues for her favours successfully or otherwise. The
irony or sarcasm which enables the shepherdess
to hold her own in the encounter is far removed from
the simplicity of popular poetry. The *Leys d'Amors*
mentions other forms of the same *genre* such as
vaqueira (cowherd), *auqueira* (goose girl), of which
a specimen of the first-named alone has survived.
Of equal interest is the *alba* or dawn-song, in which
the word *alba* reappeared as a refrain in each verse ;
the subject of the poem is the parting of the lovers
at the dawn, the approach of which is announced
by a watchman or by some faithful friend who has
undertaken to guard their meeting-place throughout the night. The counterpart of this form, the
serena, does not appear until late in the history of
Provençal lyric poetry ; in the *serena* the lover

c

longs for the approach of evening, which is to unite him with his beloved.

Other forms of minor importance were the *comjat* in which a troubadour bids a lady a final farewell, and the *escondig* or justification in which the lover attempts to excuse his behaviour to a lady whose anger he had aroused. The troubled state of his feelings might find expression in the *descort* (discord), in which each stanza showed a change of metre and melody. The *descort* of Raimbaut de Vaqueiras is written in five dialects, one for each stanza, and the last and sixth stanza of the poem gives two lines to each dialect, which Babel of strange sounds is intended, he says, to show how entirely his lady's heart has changed towards him. The *ballata* and the *estampida* were dance-songs, but very few examples survive. Certain love letters also remain to us, but as these are written in rimed couplets and in narrative style, they can hardly be classified as lyric poetry.

In conclusion, a word must be said concerning the dispute between two schools of stylists, which is one of the most interesting points in the literary history of the troubadours.[16] From the earliest times we find two poetical schools in opposition, the *trobar clus* (also known as *car, ric, oscur, sotil, cobert*), the obscure, or close, subtle style of composition, and the *trobar clar* (*leu, leugier, plan*), the clear, light, easy, straightforward style. Two or three causes may have combined to favour the development of obscure writing. The theme of love with which the *chanso* dealt is a subject by no means inexhaustible ; there was a continual struggle to revivify the well-worn tale by means of strange turns of expression, by the use of unusual adjectives and forced metaphor, by the discovery of difficult rimes (*rimes cars*) and stanza schemes of extraordinary complexity. Marcabrun asserts, possibly in jest, that he could not always understand his own poems. A further and possibly an earlier cause of obscurity in expression was the fact that the *chanso* was a love song addressed to a married lady ; and though in many cases it was the fact that the poem embodied compliments purely conventional, however exaggerated to our ideas, yet the further fact remains that the sentiments expressed might as easily be those of veritable passion, and, in view of a husband's existence, obscurity had a utility of its own. This point Guiraut de Bornelh advances as an objection to the use of the easy style : " I should like to send my song to my lady, if I should find a messenger ; but if I made another my spokesman, I fear she would blame me. For there is no sense in making another speak out what one wishes to conceal and keep to oneself." The habit of alluding to the lady addressed under a *senhal*, or pseudonym, in the course of the poem, is evidence for a need of privacy, though this custom was also conventionalised, and we find men as well as women alluded to under a *senhal*. It was not always the fact that the *senhal* was an open secret, although in many cases, where a high-born dame desired to boast of the accomplished troubadour in her service, his poems would naturally secure the widest publication which she could procure. A further reason for complexity of composition is given by the troubadour Peire d'Auvergne : "He is pleasing and agreeable to me who proceeds to sing with words shut up and obscure, to which a man is afraid to do violence." The "violence" apprehended is that of the *joglar*, who might garble a song in the performance of it, if he had not the memory or industry to learn it perfectly, and Peire d'Alvernhe (1158-80) commends compositions so constructed that the disposition of the rimes will prevent the interpolation of topical allusions or careless altercation. The similar safeguard of Dante's *terza rima* will occur to every student.

The social conditions again under which troubadour poetry was produced, apart from the limitations of its subject matter, tended to foster an obscure and highly artificial diction. This obscurity was attained, as we have said, by elevation and preciosity of style, and was not the result of con-

fusion of thought. Guiraut de Bornelh tells us
his method in a passage worth quoting in the
original—

> Mas per melhs assire
> mon chan,
> vau cercan
> bos motz en fre
> que son tuit cargat e ple
> d'us estranhs sens naturals ;
> mas no sabon tuich de cals.

" But for the better foundation of my song I keep
on the watch for words good on the rein (*i.e.* tract-
able like horses), which are all loaded (like pack
horses) and full of a meaning which is unusual,
and yet is wholly theirs (*naturals*) ; but it is not
everyone that knows what that meaning is." [17]

Difficulty was thus intentional ; in the case of
several troubadours it affected the whole of their
writing, no matter what the subject matter. They
desired not to be understood of the people. Dean
Gaisford's reputed address to his divinity lecture
illustrates the attitude of those troubadours who
affected the *trobar clus* : ' Gentlemen, a knowledge
of Greek will enable you to read the oracles of God
in the original and to look down from the heights
of scholarship upon the vulgar herd." The inevitable reaction occurred, and a movement in the
opposite direction was begun ; of this movement
the most distinguished supporter was the trouba-

dour, Guiraut de Bornelh. He had been one of the most successful exponents of the *trobar clus*, and afterwards supported the cause of the *trobar clar*. Current arguments for either cause are set forth in the *tenso* between Guiraut de Bornelh and Linhaure (pseudonym for the troubadour Raimbaut d'Aurenga).

(1) I should like to know, G. de Bornelh, why, and for what reason, you keep blaming the obscure style. Tell me if you prize so highly that which is common to all ? For then would all be equal.

(2) Sir Linhaure, I do not take it to heart if each man composes as he pleases ; but judge that song is more loved and prized which is made easy and simple, and do not be vexed at my opinion.

(3) Guiraut, I do not like my songs to be so confused, that the base and good, the small and great be appraised alike ; my poetry will never be praised by fools, for they have no understanding nor care for what is more precious and valuable.

(4) Linhaure, if I work late and turn my rest into weariness for that reason (to make my songs simple), does it seem that I am afraid of work ? Why compose if you do not want all to understand ? Song brings no other advantage.

(5) Guiraut, provided that I produce what is best at all times, I care not if it be not so widespread ; commonplaces are no good for the ap-

preciative—that is why gold is more valued than salt, and with song it is even the same.

It is obvious that the disputants are at cross purposes ; the object of writing poetry, according to the one, is to please a small circle of highly trained admirers by the display of technical skill. Guiraut de Bornelh, on the other hand, believes that the poet should have a message for the people, and that even the fools should be able to understand its purport. He adds the further statement that composition in the easy style demands no less skill and power than is required for the production of obscurity. This latter is a point upon which he repeatedly insists : " The troubadour who makes his meaning clear is just as clever as he who cunningly conjoins words." " My opinion is that it is not in obscure but in clear composition that toil is involved." Later troubadours of renown supported his arguments ; Raimon de Miraval (1168-1180) declares : " Never should obscure poetry be praised, for it is composed only for a price, compared with sweet festal songs, easy to learn, such as I sing." So, too, pronounces the Italian Lanfranc Cigala (1241-1257) : " I could easily compose an obscure, subtle poem if I wished ; but no poem should be so concealed beneath subtlety as not to be clear as day. For knowledge is of small value if clearness does not bring light ; obscurity has ever been regarded as death, and brightness as life." The fact is thus sufficiently demonstrated that these two styles existed in opposition, and that any one troubadour might practise both.

Enough has now been said to show that troubadour lyric poetry, regarded as literature, would soon produce a surfeit, if read in bulk. It is essentially a literature of artificiality and polish. Its importance consists in the fact that it was the first literature to emphasise the value of form in poetry, to formulate rules, and, in short, to show that art must be based upon scientific knowledge. The work of the troubadours in these respects left an indelible impression upon the general course of European literature.

CHAPTER IV

THE EARLY TROUBADOURS

THE earliest troubadour known to us is William IX., Count of Poitiers (1071-1127) who led an army of thirty thousand men to the unfortunate crusade of 1101. He lived an adventurous and often an unedifying life, and seems to have been a jovial sensualist caring little what kind of reputation he might obtain in the eyes of the world about him. William of Malmesbury gives an account of him which is the reverse of respectable. His poems, of which twelve survive, are, to some extent, a reflection of this character, and present a mixture of coarseness and delicate sentiment which are in strangely discordant contrast. His versification is of an early type; the principle of tripartition, which became predominant in troubadour poetry at a later date, is hardly perceptible in his poems. The chief point of interest in them is the fact that their comparative perfection of form implies a long anterior course of development for troubadour poetry, while we also find him employing, though in undeveloped form, the chief ideas which afterwards became commonplaces among the troubadours. The half mystical

41

exaltation inspired by love is already known to William IX. as *joi*, and he is acquainted with the service of love under feudal conditions. The conventional attitudes of the lady and the lover are also taken for granted, the lady disdainful and unbending, the lover timid and relying upon his patience. The lady is praised for her outward qualities, her " kindly welcome, her gracious and pleasing look " and love for her is considered to be the inspiration of nobility in the lover. But these ideas are not carried to the extravagant lengths to which later poets pushed them ; William's sensual leanings are enough to counterbalance any tendency to such exaggeration. The conventional opening of a love poem by a description of spring is also in evidence ; in short, the commonplaces, the technical language and formulæ of later Provençal lyrics were in existence during the age of this first troubadour.

Next in point of time is the troubadour Cercamon, of whom we know very little ; his poems, as we have them, seem to fall between the years 1137 and 1152 ; one of them is a lament upon the death of William X. of Aquitaine, the son of the notorious Count of Poitiers, and another alludes to the marriage of Eleanor of Aquitaine, the daughter of William X. According to the Provençal biography he was the instructor of a more interesting and original trouba-

dour Marcabrun, whose active life extended from
1150 to 1195. Many of his poems are extremely
obscure; he was one of the first to affect the *trobar
clus*. He was also the author of violent invectives
against the passion of love—

> Que anc non amet neguna
> Ni d'autra no fon amatz—

"who never loved any woman nor was loved
of any." This aversion to the main theme of
troubadour poetry is Marcabrun's most striking
characteristic.

> Amors es mout de mal avi;
> Mil homes a mortz ses glavi;
> Dieus non fetz tant fort gramavi.

"Love is of a detestable lineage; he has killed
thousands of men without a sword. God has
created no more terrible enchanter." These invectives may have been the outcome of personal dis-
appointment; the theory has also been advanced
that the troubadour idea of love had not yet secured
universal recognition, and that Marcabrun is one
who strove to prevent it from becoming the dominant
theme of lyric poetry. His best known poem was
the "Starling," which consists of two parts, an
unusual form of composition. In the first part
the troubadour sends the starling to his love to
reproach her for unfaithfulness, and to recommend

himself to her favour; the bird returns, and in the second part offers excuses from the lady and brings an invitation from her to a meeting the next day. Marcabrun knows the technical terms *cortesia* and *mesura*, which he defines: *mesura*, self-control or moderation, "consists in nicety of speech, courtesy in loving. He may boast of courtesy who can maintain moderation." The poem concludes with a dedication to Jaufre Rudel—

> Lo vers e'l son vueill envier
> A'n Jaufre Rudel outra mar.

"The words and the tune I wish to send to Jaufre Rudel beyond the sea."

This was the troubadour whom Petrarch has made famous—

> Jaufre Rudel che usò la vela e'l remo
> A cercar la sua morte.

His romantic story is as follows in the words of the Provençal biography: "Jaufre Rudel of Blaya was a very noble man, the Prince of Blaya; he fell in love with the Countess of Tripoli, though he had never seen her, for the good report that he had of her from the pilgrims who came from Antioch, and he made many poems concerning her with good tunes but poor words.[18] And from desire to see her, he took the cross and went to sea. And in the ship great illness came upon him so that

those who were with him thought that he was dead
in the ship ; but they succeeded in bringing him
to Tripoli, to an inn, as one dead. And it was
told to the countess, and she came to him, to his
bed, and took him in her arms ; and he knew that
she was the countess, and recovering his senses, he
praised God and gave thanks that his life had
been sustained until he had seen her ; and then he
died in the lady's arms. And she gave him honourable burial in the house of the Temple, and then,
on that day, she took the veil for the grief that she
had for him and for his death." Jaufre's poems
contain many references to a " distant love " which
he will never see, " for his destiny is to love without
being loved." Those critics who accept the truth of
the story regard Melisanda, daughter of Raimon I.,
Count of Tripoli, as the heroine ; but the biography
must be used with great caution as a historical
source, and the mention of the house of the order
of Templars in which Jaufre is said to have been
buried raises a difficulty ; it was erected in 1118,
and in the year 1200 the County of Tripoli was
merged in that of Antioch ; of the Rudels of Blaya,
historically known to us, there is none who falls
reasonably within these dates. The probability is
that the constant references in Jaufre's poems to
an unknown distant love, and the fact of his crusading expedition to the Holy Land, formed in con-

junction the nucleus of the legend which grew
round his name, and which is known to all readers
of Carducci, Uhland and Heine.

Contemporary with Jaufre Rudel was Bernard
de Ventadour, one of the greatest names in Provençal
poetry. According to the biography, which betrays
its untrustworthiness by contradicting the facts of
history, Bernard was the son of the furnace stoker
at the castle of Ventadour, under the Viscount
Ebles II., himself a troubadour and a patron of
troubadours. It was from the viscount that
Bernard received instruction in the troubadours'
art, and to his patron's interest in his talents he
doubtless owed the opportunities which he enjoyed
of learning to read and write, and of making acquaint-
ance with such Latin authors as were currently
read, or with the anthologies and books of " sen-
tences " then used for instruction in Latin. He
soon outstripped his patron, to whose wife, Agnes
de Montluçon, his early poems were addressed.
His relations with the lady and with his patron were
disturbed by the *lauzengiers*, the slanderers, the
envious, and the backbiters of whom troubadours
constantly complain, and he was obliged to leave
Ventadour. He went to the court of Eleanor of
Aquitaine, the granddaughter of the first troubadour, Guillaume IX. of Poitiers, who by tradition
and temperament was a patroness of troubadours,

many of whom sang her praises. She had been
divorced from Louis VII. of France in 1152, and
married Henry, Duke of Normandy, afterwards
King of England in the same year. There Bernard
may have remained until 1154, in which year
Eleanor went to England as Queen. Whether
Bernard followed her to England is uncertain ; the
personal allusions in his poems are generally scanty,
and the details of his life are correspondingly obscure.
But one poem seems to indicate that he may have
crossed the Channel. He says that he has kept
silence for two years, but that the autumn season
impels him to sing ; in spite of his love, his lady will
not deign to reply to him : but his devotion is
unchanged and she may sell him or give him away
if she pleases. She does him wrong in failing to call
him to her chamber that he may remove her shoes
humbly upon his knees, when she deigns to stretch
forth her foot. He then continues [19]

> Faitz es lo vers totz a randa,
> Si que motz no y descapduelha.
> outra la terra normanda
> part la fera mar prionda ;
> e si·m suy de midons lunhans.
> ves si·m tira cum diamans,
> la belha cui dieus defenda.
>
> Si·l reys engles el dux normans
> o vol, ieu la veirai, abans
> que l'iverns nos sobreprenda.

" The *vers* has been composed fully so that not
a word is wanting, beyond the Norman land and
the deep wild sea ; and though I am far from my
lady, she attracts me like a magnet, the fair one
whom may God protect. If the English king and
Norman duke will, I shall see her before the winter
surprise us."

How long Bernard remained in Normandy, we
cannot conjecture. He is said to have gone to the
court of Raimon V., Count of Toulouse, a well-
known patron of the troubadours. On Raimon's
death in 1194, Bernard, who must himself have
been growing old, retired to the abbey of Dalon
in his native province of Limousin, where he died.
He is perhaps more deeply inspired by the true
spirit of lyric poetry than any other troubadour ;
he insists that love is the only source of song ;
poetry to be real, must be lived.

> Non es meravelha s'ieu chan
> mielhs de nulh autre chantador ;
> que plus mi tra·l cors ves amor
> e mielhs sui faitz a son coman.

" It is no wonder if I sing better than any other
singer ; for my heart draws me more than others
towards love, and I am better made for his com-
mandments." Hence Bernard gave fuller expression
than any other troubadour to the ennobling power
of love, as the only source of real worth and nobility.

The subject speedily became exhausted, and ingenuity did but increase the conventionality of its
treatment. But in Bernard's hands it retains its
early freshness and sincerity. The description of
the seasons of the year as impelling the troubadour
to song was, or became, an entirely conventional
and expected opening to a *chanso*; but in Bernard's
case these descriptions were marked by the observation and feeling of one who had a real love for the
country and for nature, and the contrast or comparison between the season of the year and his own
feelings is of real lyrical value. The opening with
the description of the lark is famous—

> Quant vey la lauzeta mover
> De joi sas alas contral rai,
> que s'oblida e·s laissa cazer
> per la doussor qu'al cor li vai,
> ai ! tan grans enveia m'en ve
> de cui qu'eu veya jauzion !
> meravilhas ai, quar desse
> lo cor de dezirier no·m fon.

" When I see the lark flutter with joy towards
the sun, and forget himself and sing for the sweetness that comes to his heart ; alas, such envy comes
upon me of all that I see rejoicing, I wonder that
my heart does not melt forthwith with desire." [20]

At the same time Bernard's style is simple and
clear, though he shows full mastery of the complex
stanza form ; to call him the Wordsworth of the

D

troubadour world is to exaggerate a single point of coincidence ; but he remains the greatest of troubadour poets, as modern taste regards poetry.

Arnaut de Mareuil (1170-1200 *circa*) displays many of the characteristics which distinguished the poetry of Bernard of Ventadour ; there is the same simplicity of style and often no less reality of feeling : conventionalism had not yet become typical. Arnaut was born in Périgord of poor parents, and was brought up to the profession of a scribe or notary. This profession he soon abandoned, and his " good star," to quote the Provençal biography, led him to the court of Adelaide, daughter of Raimon V. of Toulouse, who had married in 1171 Roger II., Viscount of Béziers. There he soon rose into high repute ; at first he is said to have denied his authorship of the songs which he composed in honour of his mistress, but eventually he betrayed himself and was recognised as a troubadour of high merit, and definitely installed as the singer of Adelaide. The story is improbable, as the troubadour's rewards naturally depended upon the favour of his patrons to him personally ; it is probably an instance of the manner in which the biographies founded fictions upon a very meagre substratum of fact, the fact in this instance being a passage in which Arnaut declares his timidity in singing the praise of so great a beauty as Adelaide.

Mas grans paors m'o tol e grans temensa,
Qu'ieu non aus dir, dona, qu'ieu chant de vos.

" But great fear and great apprehension comes upon
me, so that I dare not tell you, lady, that it is I
who sing of you."

Arnaut seems to have introduced a new poetical
genre into Provençal literature, the love-letter.
He says that the difficulty of finding a trustworthy
messenger induced him to send a letter sealed with
his own ring ; the letter is interesting for the description of feminine beauty which it contains :
" my heart, that is your constant companion,
comes to me as your messenger and portrays for
me your noble, graceful form, your fair light-brown
hair, your brow whiter than the lily, your gay
laughing eyes, your straight well-formed nose,
your fresh complexion, whiter and redder than any
flower, your little mouth, your fair teeth, whiter
than pure silver, . . . your fair white hands with
the smooth and slender fingers " ; in short, a picture
which shows that troubadour ideas of beauty were
much the same as those of any other age. Arnaut
was eventually obliged to leave Béziers, owing,
it is said, to the rivalry of Alfonso II. of Aragon,
who may have come forward as a suitor for Adelaide
after Roger's death in 1194. The troubadour betook
himself to the court of William VIII., Count of
Montpelier, where he probably spent the rest of

his life. The various allusions in his poems cannot always be identified, and his career is only known to us in vague outline. Apart from the love-letter, he was, if not the initiator, one of the earliest writers of the type of didactic poem known as *ensenhamen*, an "instruction" containing observations upon the manners and customs of his age, with precepts for the observance of morality and right conduct such as should be practised by the ideal character. Arnaut, after a lengthy and would-be learned introduction, explains that each of the three estates, the knights, the clergy and the citizens, have their special and appropriate virtues. The emphasis with which he describes the good qualities of the citizen class, a compliment unusual in the aristocratic poetry of the troubadours, may be taken as confirmation of the statement concerning his own parentage which we find in his biography.

CHAPTER V

THE CLASSICAL PERIOD

WE now reach a group of three troubadours whom Dante [21] selected as typical of certain characteristics : " Bertran de Born sung of arms, Arnaut Daniel of love, and Guiraut de Bornelh of uprightness, honour and virtue." The last named, who was a contemporary (1175-1220 *circa*) and compatriot of Arnaut de Marueil, is said in his biography to have enjoyed so great a reputation that he was known as the " Master of the Troubadours." This title is not awarded to him by any other troubadour ; the jealousy constantly prevailing between the troubadours is enough to account for their silence on this point. But his reputation is fairly attested by the number of his poems which have survived and by the numerous MSS. in which they are preserved ; when troubadours were studied as classics in the thirteenth and fourteenth centuries, Guiraut's poems were so far in harmony with the moralising tendency of that age that his posthumous reputation was certainly as great as any that he enjoyed in his life-time.

Practically nothing is known of his life ; allusions in his poems lead us to suppose that he spent some time in Spain at the courts of Navarre, Castile and Aragon. The real interests of his work are literary and ethical. To his share in the controversy concerning the *trobar clus*, the obscure and difficult style of composition, we have already alluded. Though in the *tenso* with Linhaure, Guiraut expresses his preference for the simple and intelligible style, it must be said that the majority of his poems are far from attaining this ideal. Their obscurity, however, is often due rather to the difficulty of the subject matter than to any intentional attempt at preciosity of style. He was one of the first troubadours who attempted to analyse the effects of love from a psychological standpoint ; his analysis often proceeds in the form of a dialogue with himself, an attempt to show the hearer by what methods he arrived at his conclusions. " How is it, in the name of God, that when I wish to sing, I weep ? Can the reason be that love has conquered me ? And does love bring me no delight ? Yes, delight is mine. Then why am I sad and melancholy ? I cannot tell. I have lost my lady's favour and the delight of love has no more sweetness for me. Had ever a lover such misfortune ? But am I a lover ? No ! Have I ceased to love passionately ? No ! Am I then a lover ? Yes, if my lady would suffer my love." Guiraut's moral *sirventes* are reprobations of the decadence of his age. He saw a gradual decline of the true spirit of chivalry. The great lords were fonder of war and pillage than of poetry and courtly state. He had himself suffered from the change, if his biographer is to be believed; the Viscount of Limoges had plundered and burnt his house. He compares the evils of his own day with the splendours of the past, and asks whether the accident of birth is the real source of nobility; a man must be judged by himself and his acts and not by the rank of his forefathers; these were the sentiments that gained him a mention in the Fourth Book of Dante's *Convivio*.[22]

The question why Dante should have preferred Arnaut Daniel to Guiraut de Bornelh [23] has given rise to much discussion. The solution turns upon Dante's conception of style, which is too large a problem for consideration here. Dante preferred the difficult and artificial style of Arnaut to the simple style of the opposition school; from Arnaut he borrowed the sestina form; and at the end of the canto he puts the well-known lines, "Ieu sui Arnaut, que plor e vau cantan," into the troubadour's mouth. We know little of Arnaut's life; he was a noble of Riberac in Périgord. The biography relates an incident in his life which is said to have taken place at the court of Richard Cœur de Lion.

A certain troubadour had boasted before the king that he could compose a better poem than Arnaut. The latter accepted the challenge and the king confined the poets to their rooms for a certain time at the end of which they were to recite their composition before him. Arnaut's inspiration totally failed him, but from his room he could hear his rival singing as he rehearsed his own composition. Arnaut was able to learn his rival's poem by heart, and when the time of trial came he asked to be allowed to sing first, and performed his opponent's song, to the wrath of the latter, who protested vigorously. Arnaut acknowledged the trick, to the great amusement of the king.

Preciosity and artificiality reach their height in Arnaut's poems, which are, for that reason, excessively difficult. Enigmatic constructions, wordplays, words used in forced senses, continual alliteration and difficult rimes produced elaborate form and great obscurity of meaning. The following stanza may serve as an example—

> L'aur' amara   fa·ls bruels brancutz
> clarzir   que·l dous espeys' ab fuelhs,
> e·ls letz   becxs   dels auzels ramencx
> te balbs e mutz   pars   e non pars.
> per qu'ieu m'esfortz   de far e dir plazers
> A manhs ? per ley   qui m'a virat bas d'aut,
> don tem morir   si·ls afans no·m asoma.

" The bitter breeze makes light the bosky boughs
which the gentle breeze makes thick with leaves,
and the joyous beaks of the birds in the branches
it keeps silent and dumb, paired and not paired.
Wherefore do I strive to say and do what is pleasing
to many ? For her, who has cast me down from
on high, for which I fear to die, if she does not end
the sorrow for me."

The answers to the seventeen rime-words which
occur in this stanza do not appear till the following
stanza, the same rimes being kept throughout
the six stanzas of the poem. To rest the listener's
ear, while he waited for the answering rimes, Arnaut
used light assonances which almost amount to rime
in some cases. The Monk of Montaudon in his
satirical *sirventes* says of Arnaut : " He has sung
nothing all his life, except a few foolish verses which
no one understands " ; and we may reasonably
suppose that Arnaut's poetry was as obscure to
many of his contemporaries as it is to us.

Dante placed Bertran de Born in hell, as a sower
of strife between father and son, and there is no need
to describe his picture of the troubadour—

> " Who held the severed member lanternwise
> And said, Ah me ! "   (*Inf.* xxviii. 119-142.)

The genius of Dante, and the poetical fame of
Bertran himself, have given him a more important

position in history than is, perhaps, entirely his due. Jaufré, the prior of Vigeois, an abbey of Saint-Martial of Limoges, is the only chronicler during the reigns of Henry II. and Richard Cœur de Lion who mentions Bertran's name. The *razos* prefixed to some of his poems by way of explanation are the work of an anonymous troubadour (possibly Uc de Saint-Circ); they constantly misinterpret the poems they attempt to explain, confuse names and events, and rather exaggerate the part played by Bertran himself. Besides these sources we have the cartulary of Dalon, or rather the extracts made from it by Guignières in 1680 (the original has been lost), which give us information about Bertran's family and possessions. From these materials, and from forty-four or forty-five poems which have come down to us, the poet's life can be reconstructed.

Bertran de Born's estates were situated on the borders of Limousin and Périgord. The family was ancient and honourable; from the cartulary Bertran appears to have been born about 1140; we find him, with his brother Constantin, in possession of the castle of Hautefort, which seems to have been a strong fortress; the lands belonging to the family were of no great extent, and the income accruing from them was but scanty. In 1179 Bertran married one Raimonde, of whom nothing is known, except that she bore him at least two sons. In 1192 he lost this first wife, and again married a certain Philippe. His warlike and turbulent character was the natural outcome of the conditions under which he lived ; the feudal system divided the country into a number of fiefs, the boundaries of which were ill defined, while the lords were constantly at war with one another. All owed allegiance to the Duke of Aquitaine, the Count of Poitou, but his suzerainty was, in the majority of cases, rather a name than a reality. These divisions were further accentuated by political events ; in 1152 Henry II., Count of Anjou and Maine, married Eleanor, the divorced wife of Louis VII. of France, and mistress of Aquitaine. Henry became king of England two years later, and his rule over the barons of Aquitaine, which had never been strict, became the more relaxed owing to his continual absence in England.

South of Aquitaine proper the dominions of the Count of Toulouse stretched from the Garonne to the Alps ; this potentate was also called the Duke of Narbonne, and was not disposed to recognise the suzerainty of the Duke of Aquitaine. But in 1167 Alfonso II., King of Aragon and Count of Barcelona, had inherited Provence, to which the Duke of Toulouse laid claim. Henry and Alfonso thus became natural allies, and the power of Alfonso in Aragon and Catalonia, was able to keep in check any serious attempt that the Count of Toulouse might have meditated on Aquitaine. On the other hand, Henry had also to deal with a formidable adversary in the person of the French king, his lawful suzerain in France. Louis VII. (or Philippe Auguste) was able to turn the constant revolts that broke out in Aquitaine to his own ends.

These circumstances are sufficient to account for the warlike nature of Bertran de Born's poetry. The first *sirventes* which can be dated with certainty belongs to 1811, and is a call to the allies of Raimon V., Count of Toulouse, to aid their master against the King of Aragon. What Bertran's personal share in the campaign was, we do not know. He was soon involved in a quarrel with his brother Constantin, with whom he held the castle of Hautefort in common. Constantin was driven out and succeeded in persuading the Count of Limoges and Richard, Duke of Aquitaine, to help him. Richard, however, was occupied elsewhere, and Bertran survived all attacks upon the castle. In 1182 he went to the court of Henry II., during a temporary lull in the wars around him ; there he proceeded to pay court to the Princess Matilda, daughter of Henry II., whose husband, Henry of Saxony, was then on a pilgrimage. He also took part in the political affairs of the time. Henry II.'s eldest son, Henry " the young king," had been crowned in 1170 at Westminster, and was anxious to have something more than the title, seeing that his brother Richard was Duke of Aquitaine, Count of Poitou, and practically an independent sovereign. Bertran had not forgotten Richard's action against him on behalf of his brother Constantin, and was, moreover, powerfully attracted by the open and generous nature of the young king. He therefore took his side, and on his return to Limousin became the central point of the league which was formed against Richard. Henry II. succeeded in reconciling his two sons, the young Henry receiving pecuniary compensation in lieu of political power. But the young Henry seems to have been really moved by Bertran's reproaches, and at length revolted against his father and attacked his brother Richard. While he was in Turenne, the young king fell sick and died on June 11, 1183. Bertran lamented his loss in two famous poems, and soon felt the material effects of it. On June 29, Richard and the King of Aragon arrived before Hautefort, which surrendered after a week's resistance. Richard restored the castle to Constantin, but Bertran regained possession, as is related in the second biography.

Henceforward, Bertran remained faithful to Richard, and directed his animosity chiefly against the King of Aragon. At the same time it appears

that he would have been equally pleased with any
war, which would have brought profit to himself,
and attempted to excite Richard against his father,
Henry II. This project came to nothing, but war
broke out between Richard and the French king;
a truce of two years was concluded, and again
broken by Richard. The Church, however, inter-
fered with its efforts to organise the Third Crusade,
which called from Bertran two *sirventes* in honour
of Conrad, son of the Marquis of Montferrat, who
was defending Tyre against Saladin. Bertran remained at home in Limousin during this Crusade;
his means were obviously insufficient to enable him
to share in so distant a campaign; other, and for
him, equally cogent reasons for remaining at home
may be gathered from his poems. There followed
the quarrels between Richard and the French
king, the return to France of the latter, and
finally Richard's capture on the Illyrian coast
and his imprisonment by Henry VI. of Austria,
which terminated in 1194. Richard then came
into Aquitaine, his return being celebrated by
two poems from Bertran.

The Provençal biography informs us that Bertran
finally became a monk in the Order of Citeaux.
The convent where he spent his last years was the
abbey of Dalon, near Hautefort. The cartulary
mentions his name at various intervals from 1197

to 1202. In 1215 we have the entry "*octava candela in sepulcro ponitur pro Bernardo de Born : cera tres solidos empta est.*" This is the only notice of the poet's death.

Dante perhaps exaggerated the part he played in stirring up strife between Henry II. and his sons ; modern writers go to the other extreme. Bertran is especially famous for his political *sirventes* and for the martial note which rings through much of his poetry. He loved war both for itself and for the profits which it brought : "The powerful are more generous and open-handed when they have war than when they have peace." The troubadour's two *planhs* upon the "young king's" death are inspired by real feeling, and the story of his reconciliation with Henry after the capture of his castle can hardly have been known to Dante, who would surely have modified his judgment upon the troubadour if he had remembered that scene as related by the biography. "Sir Bertran was summoned with all his people to King Henry's tent, who received him very harshly and said, "Bertran, you declared that you never needed more than half your senses ; it seems that to-day you will want the whole of them." "Sire," said Bertran, "it is true that I said so and I said nothing but the truth." The king replied, "Then you seem to me to have lost your senses entirely." "I have indeed lost them," said Bertran. " And how ? " asked the king. " Sire, on the day that the noble king, your son, died, I lost sense, knowledge and understanding." When the king heard Bertran speak of his son with tears, he was deeply moved and overcome with grief. On recovering himself he cried, weeping, " Ah, Bertran, rightly did you lose your senses for my son, for there was no one in the world whom he loved as you. And for love of him, not only do I give you your life, but also your castle and your goods, and I add with my love five hundred silver marks to repair the loss which you have suffered."

The narrative is unhistorical; Henry II. was not present in person at the siege of Hautefort ; but the fact is certain that he regarded Bertran as the chief sower of discord in his family.

Mention must now be made of certain troubadours who were less important than the three last mentioned, but are of interest for various reasons.

Raimbaut d'Aurenga, Count of Orange from 1150-1173, is interesting rather by reason of his relations with other troubadours than for his own achievements in the troubadours' art. He was a follower of the precious, artificial and obscure style, and prided himself upon his skill in the combination of difficult rimes and the repetition of equivocal rimes (the same word used in different senses or grammatical forms). " Since Adam ate the apple," he says, " there is no poet, loud as he may proclaim himself, whose art is worth a turnip compared with mine." Apart from these mountebank tricks and certain mild " conceits " (his lady's smile, for instance, makes him happier than the smile of four hundred angels could do), the chief characteristic of his poetry is his constant complaints of slanderers who attempt to undermine his credit with his lady. But he seems to have aroused a passion in the heart of a poetess, who expressed her feelings in words which contrast strongly with Raimbaut's vapid sentimentalities.

This was Beatrice, Countess of Die and the wife of Count William of Poitiers. The names, at least, of seventeen poetesses are known to us and of these the Countess of Die is the most famous. Like the rest of her sex who essayed the troubadour's art, the Countess knows nothing of difficult rhymes or obscurity of style. Simplicity and sincerity are the keynotes of her poetry. The troubadour sang because he was a professional poet, but the lady who composed poetry did so from love of the art or from the inspiration of feeling and therefore felt no need of meretricious adornment for her song. The five poems of the Countess which remain to us show that her sentiment for Raimbaut was real and deep. " I am glad to know that the man I love is the worthiest in the world ; may God give

E

great joy to the one who first brought me to him : may he trust only in me, whatever slanders be reported to him : for often a man plucks the rod with which he beats himself. The woman who values her good name should set her love upon a noble and valiant knight : when she knows his worth, let her not hide her love. When a woman loves thus openly, the noble and worthy speak of her love only with sympathy." Raimbaut, however, did not reciprocate these feelings : in a *tenso* with the countess he shows his real sentiments while excusing his conduct. He assures her that he has avoided her only because he did not wish to provide slanderers with matter for gossip ; to which the Countess replies that his care for her reputation is excessive. Peire Rogier whose poetical career lies between the years 1160 and 1180, also spent some time at Raimbaut's court. He belonged to Auvergne by birth and was attached to the court of Ermengarde of Narbonne for some years : here there is no doubt that we have a case of a troubadour in an official position and nothing more : possibly Peire Rogier's tendency to preaching—he had been educated for the church—was enough to stifle any sentiment on the lady's side. On leaving Narbonne, he visited Raimbaut at Orange and afterwards travelled to Spain and Toulouse, finally entering a monastery where he ended his life.

Auvergne produced a far more important troubadour in the person of Peire d'Auvergne, whose work
extended from about 1158 to 1180 ; he was thus
more or less contemporary with Guiraut de Bornelh
and Bernart de Ventadour. He was, according
to the biography, the son of a citizen of Clermont-
Ferrand, and "the first troubadour, who lived
beyond the mountains (*i.e.* the Pyrenees, which,
however, Marcabrun had previously crossed) . . .
he was regarded as the best troubadour until Guiraut
de Bornelh appeared. . . . He was very proud
of his talents and despised other troubadours."
Other notices state that he was educated for an
ecclesiastical career and was at one time a canon.
He had no small idea of his own powers : " Peire
d'Auvergne," he says in his satire upon other troubadours " has such a voice that he can sing in all
tones and his melodies are sweet and pleasant :
he is master of his art, if he would but put a little
clarity into his poems, which are difficult to understand." The last observation is entirely correct :
his poems are often very obscure. Peire travelled,
in the pursuit of his profession, to the court of
Sancho III. of Castile and made some stay in
Spain : he is also found at the courts of Raimon V.
of Toulouse and, like Peire Rogier, at Narbonne.
Among his poems, two are especially well known.
In a love poem he makes the nightingale his

messenger, as Marcabrun had used the starling and as others used the swallow or parrot. But in comparison with Marcabrun, Peire d'Auvergne worked out the idea with a far more delicate poetical touch. The other poem is a *sirventes* which is of interest as being the first attempt at literary satire among the troubadours ; the satire is often rather of a personal than of a literary character ; the following quotations referring to troubadours already named will show Peire's ideas of literary criticism. " Peire Rogier sings of love without restraint and it would befit him better to carry the psalter in the church or to bear the lights with the great burning candles. Guiraut de Bornelh is like a sun-bleached cloth with his thin miserable song which might suit an old Norman water-carrier. Bernart de Ventadour is even smaller than Guiraut de Bornelh by a thumb's length ; but he had a servant for his father who shot well with the long bow while his mother tended the furnace." The satiric *sirventes* soon found imitators : the Monk of Montaudon produced a similar composition. Like many other troubadours, Peire ended his life in a monastery. To this period of his career probably belong his religious poems of which we shall have occasion to speak later.

We have already observed that the Church contributed members, though with some reluctance, to the ranks of the troubadours. One of the most striking figures of the kind is the Monk of Montaudon (1180-1200) : the satirical power of his *sirventes* attracted attention, and he gained much wealth at the various courts which he visited ; this he used for the benefit of his priory. He enjoyed the favour of Philippe Auguste II. of France, of Richard Cœur de Lion and of Alfonso II. of Aragon, with that of many smaller nobles. The biography says of him, " E fo faitz seigner de la cort del Puoi Santa Maria e de dar l'esparvier. Lonc temps ac la seignoria de la cort del Puoi, tro que la cortz se perdet." " He was made president of the court of Puy Sainte Marie and of awarding the sparrow-hawk. For a long time he held the presidency of the court of Puy, until the court was dissolved." The troubadour Richard de Barbezieux refers to this court, which seems to have been a periodical meeting attended by the nobles and troubadours of Southern France. Tournaments and poetical contests were held ; the sparrow-hawk or falcon placed on a pole is often mentioned as the prize awarded to the tournament victor. Tennyson's version of the incident in his " Geraint and Enid " will occur to every reader. The monk's reputation must have been considerable to gain him this position. His love poems are of little importance ; his satire deals with the petty failings of mankind, for which he had a keen eye and an unsparing and sometimes cynical tongue.

> Be·m enoia, s'o auzes dire,
> Parliers quant es avols servire ;
> Et hom qui trop vol aut assire
> M'enoia, e cavals que tire.
> Et enoia·m, si Dieus m'aiut
> Joves hom quan trop port' escut,
> Que negun colp no i a agut,
> Capela et mongue barbut,
> E lauzengier bec esmolut.

" These vex me greatly, if I may say so, language when it is base servility, and a man who wishes too high a place (at table) and a charger which is put to drawing carts. And, by my hope of salvation, I am vexed by a young man who bears too openly a shield which has never received a blow, by a chaplain and monk wearing beards and by the sharp beak of the slanderer." The monk's satire upon other troubadours is stated by himself to be a continuation of that by Peire d'Auvergne ; the criticism is, as might be expected, personal. Two *tensos* deal with the vanities of women, especially the habit of painting the face : in one of them the dispute proceeds before God as judge, between the poet and the women : the scene of the other is laid in Paradise and the interlocutors are the Almighty and the poet, who, represents that self-adornment is a habit inherent in female nature. In neither poem is reverence a prominent feature.

One of the most extraordinary figures in the whole gallery of troubadour portraits is Peire Vidal, whose career extended, roughly speaking, from 1175 to 1215. He was one of those characters who naturally become the nucleus of apocryphal stories, and how much truth there may be in some of the fantastic incidents, in which he figures as the hero, will probably never be discovered. He was undoubtedly an attractive character, for he enjoyed the favour of the most distinguished men and women of his time. He was also a poet of real power : ease and facility are characteristics of his poems as compared with the ingenious obscurity of Arnaut Daniel or Peire d'Auvergne. But there was a whimsical and fantastic strain in his character, which led him often to conjoin the functions of court-fool with those of court poet : " he was the most foolish man in the world " says his biographer. His " foolishness " also induced him to fall in love with every woman he met, and to believe that his personal attractions made him invincible.

Peire Vidal was the son of a Toulouse merchant. He began his troubadour wanderings early and at the outset of his career we find him in Catalonia, Aragon and Castile. He is then found in the service of Raimon Gaufridi Barral,[24] Viscount of

Marseilles, a bluff, genial tournament warrior and the husband of Azalais de Porcellet whose praises were sung by Folquet of Marseilles. It was Barral who was attracted by Peire's peculiar talents : his wife seems to have tolerated the troubadour from deference to her husband. Peire, however, says in one of his poems that husbands feared him more than fire or sword, and believing himself irresistible interpreted Azalais' favours as seriously meant. When he stole a kiss from her as she slept, she insisted upon Peire's departure, though her husband seems to have regarded the matter as a jest and the troubadour took refuge in Genoa. Eventually, Azalais pardoned him and he was able to return to Marseilles. Peire is said to have followed Richard Cœur de Lion on his crusade ; it was in 1190 that Richard embarked at Marseilles for the Holy Land, and as a patron of troubadours, he was no doubt personally acquainted with Peire. The troubadour, however, is said to have gone no farther than Cyprus. There he married a Greek woman and was somehow persuaded that his wife was a daughter of the Emperor of Constantinople, and that he, therefore, had a claim to the throne of Greece. He assumed royal state, added a throne to his personal possessions and began to raise a fleet for the conquest of his kingdom. How long this farce continued is unknown. Barral died in 1192 and Peire transferred

his affections to a lady of Carcassonne, Loba de
Pennautier. The biography relates that her name
Loba (wolf) induced the troubadour to approach
her in a wolf's skin, which disguise was so successful that he was attacked by a pack of dogs
and seriously mauled. Probably the story that an
outraged husband had the troubadour's tongue
cut out at an earlier period of his life contains an
equal substratum of truth. The last period of his
career was spent in Hungary and Lombardy. His
political *sirventes* show an insight into the affairs
of his age, which is in strong contrast to the whimsicality which seems to have misguided his own life.

Guillem de Cabestanh (between 1181 and 1196)
deserves mention for the story which the Provençal
biography has attached to his name, a Provençal
variation of the thirteenth century romance of
the *Châtelaine de Coucy*.[25] He belonged to the
Roussillon district, on the borders of Catalonia and
fell in love with the wife of his overlord, Raimon of
Roussillon. Margarida or Seremonda, as she is
respectively named in the two versions of the
story, was attracted by Guillem's songs, with the
result that Raimon's jealousy was aroused and
meeting the troubadour one day, when he was out
hunting, he killed him. The Provençal version
proceeds as follows : " he then took out the heart
and sent it by a squire to the castle. He caused it

to be roasted with pepper and gave it to his wife to eat. And when she had eaten it, her lord told her what it was and she lost the power of sight and hearing. And when she came to herself, she said, "my lord, you have given me such good meat that never will I eat such meat again." He made at her to strike her but she threw herself from the window and was killed. Thereupon the barons of Catalonia and Aragon, led by King Alfonso, are said to have made a combined attack upon Raimon and to have ravaged his lands, in indignation at his barbarity.

The Provençal biography, like the romance of the *Châtelain de Coucy*, belongs to the thirteenth century, and the story cannot be accepted as authentic. But the period of decadence had begun. By the close of the twelfth century the golden age of troubadour poetry was over. Guiraut de Bornelh's complaints that refinement was vanishing and that nobles were growing hard-hearted and avaricious soon became common-places in troubadour poetry. The extravagances of the previous age and the rise of a strong middle and commercial class diminished both the wealth and the influence of the nobles, while the peace of the country was further disturbed by theological disputes and by the rise of the Albigeois heresy.

CHAPTER VI

THE ALBIGEOIS CRUSADE

THE feudal society in which troubadour poetry
had flourished, and by which alone it could be
maintained, was already showing signs of decadence.
Its downfall was precipitated by the religious and
political movement, the Albigeois Crusade, which
was the first step towards the unification of France,
but which also broke up the local fiefs, destroyed
the conditions under which the troubadours had
flourished and scattered them abroad in other lands
or forced them to seek other means of livelihood.
This is not the place to discuss the origin and
the nature of the Albigeois heresy.[26] The general
opinion has almost invariably considered the
heretics as dualists and their belief as a variation
of Manicheism : but a plausible case has been
made out for regarding the heresy as a variant of
the Adoptionism which is found successively in
Armenia, in the Balkan peninsula and in Spain,
and perhaps sporadically in Italy and Germany.
Whatever its real nature was, the following facts
are clear : it was not an isolated movement, but
was in continuity with beliefs prevalent in many

other parts of Europe. It was largely a poor man's heresy and therefore emerges into the light of history only when it happens to attract aristocratic adherents or large masses of people. It was also a pre-Reformation movement and essentially in opposition to Roman Catholicism. Albi was the first head-quarters of the heresy, though Toulouse speedily rivalled its importance in this respect. The Vaudois heresy which became notorious at Lyons about the same time was a schismatic, not a heretic movement. The Vaudois objected to the profligacy and worldliness of the Roman Catholic clergy, but did not quarrel with church doctrine. The Albigenses were no less zealous than the Vaudois in reproving the church clergy and setting an example of purity and unselfishness of life. But they also differed profoundly from the church in matters of doctrine.

Upon the election of Otho as Emperor, in 1208, Germany and Rome were at peace, and Pope Innocent III. found himself at liberty to devote some attention to affairs in Southern France. He had already made some efforts to oppose the growth of heresy : his first emissaries were unable to produce the least effect and in 1208 he had sent Arnaut of Citeaux and two Cistercian monks into Southern France with full powers to act. Their efforts proved fruitless, because Philippe Auguste was no less indifferent than the provincial lords, who actually favoured the heretics in many cases ; the Roman Catholic bishops also were jealous of the pope's legates and refused to support them. Not only the laity but many of the clergy had been seduced : the heretics had translated large portions of scripture (translations which still remain to us) and constantly appealed to the scriptures in opposition to the canon laws and the immorality of Rome. They had a full parochial and diocesan organisation and were in regular communication with the heretics of other countries. It was clear that the authority of Southern France was doomed, unless some vigorous steps to assert her authority were speedily taken. " Ita per omnes terras multiplicati sunt ut grande periculum patiatur ecclesia Dei." [27] The efforts of St Dominic were followed by the murder of the papal legate, Pierre de Castelnau, in 1208, which created an excitement comparable with that aroused by the murder of Thomas à Becket, thirty-eight years before, and gave Innocent III. his opportunity. In the summer of 1209 a great army of crusaders assembled at Lyons, and Southern France was invaded by a horde composed partly of religious fanatics, of men who were anxious to gain the indulgences awarded to crusaders without the danger of a journey overseas, and of men who were simply bent on plunder. The last stage in the development of the crusade movement was thereby reached : originally begun to recover the Holy Sepulchre, it had been extended to other countries against the avowed enemies of Christianity. Now the movement was to be turned against erring members of the Christian Church and in the terms of a metaphor much abused at that period, the Crusader was not only to destroy the wolf, but to drive the vagrant sheep back into the fold.[28] Béziers and Carcassonne were captured with massacre ; Toulouse was spared upon the humiliating submission of Raimon VI., and little organised opposition was offered to the crusading forces under Simon de Montfort. The following years saw the revolt of Toulouse and the excommunication of Raimon VI. (1211), the battle of Muret in which Raimon was defeated and his supporter Pedro of Aragon, was killed (1213), the Lateran Council (1215), the siege of Toulouse and the death of Simon de Montfort (1218). The foundation of the Dominican order and of the Inquisition marked the close of the struggle.

Folquet of Marseilles is a troubadour whose life belongs to these years of turmoil. He was the son of a Genoese merchant by name Anfos, who apparently settled in Marseilles for business reasons : Genoa was in close commercial relations with the South of France during the twelfth century, as is attested by treaties concluded with Marseilles in

1138 and with Raimon of Toulouse in 1174.
Folquet (or Fulco in Latin form) seems to have
carried on his father's business and to have amused
his leisure hours by poetical composition. The
Monk of Montandon refers to him as a merchant
in his *sirventes* upon other troubadours. He is
placed in Paradise by Dante and is the only troubadour who there appears, no doubt because of his
services to the Church. His earliest poems, written
after 1180, were composed in honour of Azalais,
the lady whose favour was sought by Peire Vidal,
and to whom Folquet refers by the *senhal* of Aimant
(magnet). His poems are ingenious dissertations
upon love and we catch little trace of real feeling
in them. The stories of the jealousy of Azalais'
sister which drove Folquet to leave Marseilles are
probably apocryphal. Folquet also addressed poems
to the wife of the Count of Montpelier, the daughter
of the Emperor of Constantinople. He wrote
a fine *planh* on the death of Barral of Marseilles in
1192 and it was about this time that he resolved
to enter the church. His last poem belongs to the
year 1195. No doubt the wealth which he may
have brought to the Church as a successful merchant contributed to his advancement, but Folquet
was also an in domitably energetic character.

Unlike so many of his fellow poets, who retired
to monasteries and there lived out their lives in

seclusion, Folquet displayed special talents or special enthusiasm for the order which he joined. Of the Cistercian abbey of Toronet in the diocese of Fréjus he became abbot, and in 1205 was made Bishop of Toulouse. He then, in company with St Dominic, becomes one of the great figures of the Albigeois crusade : in 1209 he was acting with Simon de Montfort against Raimon VI., the son of his old patron and benefactor, and persuaded the count to surrender the citadel of Toulouse to de Montfort and the papal legate. He travelled in Northern France in order to stir up enthusiasm for the crusade. The legend is related that, hearing one of his love songs sung by a minstrel at Paris, he imposed penance upon himself. He helped to establish the Inquisition in Languedoc, and at the Lateran council of 1215 was the most violent opponent of Count Raimon. To enter into his history in detail during this period would be to recount a large portion of the somewhat intricate history of the crusade. Of his fanaticism, and of the cruelty with which he waged war upon the heretics, the Count Raimon Roger of Foix speaks at the Lateran council, when defending himself against the accusation of heresy.

> E dic vos de l'avesque, que tant n'es afortitz,
> qu'en la sua semblansa es Dieus e nos trazitz,
> que ab cansos messengeiras e ab motz coladitz,

dont totz hom es perdutz qui·ls canta ni los ditz,
ez ab sos reproverbis afilatz e forbitz
ez ab los nostres dos, don fo eniotglaritz,
ez ab mala doctrina es tant fort enriquitz
c'om non auza ren dire a so qu'el contraditz.
Pero cant el fo abas ni monges revestitz
en la sua abadia fo si·l lums escurzitz
qu'anc no i ac be ni pauza, tro qu'el ne fo ichitz ;
e cant fo de Tholosa avesques elegitz
per trastota la terra es tals focs espanditz
que ia mais per nulha aiga no sira escantitz ;
que plus de .D.M., que de grans que petitz,
i fe perdre las vidas é·ls cors e·ls esperitz.
Per la fe qu'ieu vos deg, als seus faitz e als ditz
ez a la captenensa sembla mielhs Antecritz
que messatges de Roma.

" And of the bishop, who is so zealous, I tell you
that in him both God and we ourselves are betrayed ;
for with lying songs and insinuating words, which
are the damnation of any who sings or speaks
them, and by his keen polished admonitions, and
by our presents wherewith he maintained himself
as *joglar*, and by his evil doctrine, he has risen so
high, that one dare say nothing to that which he
opposes. So when he was vested as abbot and
monk, was the light in his abbey put out in such
wise that therein was no comfort or rest, until that
he was gone forth from thence ; and when he was
chosen bishop of Toulouse such a fire was spread
throughout the land that never for any water will
it be quenched ; for there did he bring destruction

F

of life and body and soul upon more than fifteen
hundred of high and low.   By the faith which I
owe to you, by his deeds and his words and his
dealings, more like is he to Anti-Christ than to an
envoy of Rome."   (*Chanson de la croisade contre
les Albigeois*, v. 3309.)

Folquet died on December 25, 1231, and was
buried at the Cistercian Abbey of Grandselve,
some thirty miles north-west of Toulouse.   Such
troubadours as Guilhem Figueira and Peire Cardenal,
who inveighed against the action of the Church
during the crusade, say nothing of him, and upon
their silence and that of the biography as regards
his ecclesiastical life the argument has been founded
that Folquet the troubadour and Folquet the
bishop were two different persons.   There is no
evidence to support this theory.   Folquet's poems
enjoyed a high reputation.   The minnesinger,
Rudolf, Count of Neuenberg (end of the twelfth
century) imitated him, as also did the Italians
Rinaldo d'Aquino and Jacopo da Lentino.

The troubadours as a rule stood aloof from the
religious quarrels of the age.   But few seem to
have joined the crusaders, as Perdigon did.   Most
of their patrons were struggling for their existence :
when the invaders succeeded in establishing themselves, they had no desire for court poetry.   The
troubadour's occupation was gone, and those who

wished for an audience were obliged to seek beyond the borders of France. Hence it is somewhat remarkable to find the troubadour Raimon de Miraval, of Carcassonne, continuing to sing, as though perfect tranquillity prevailed. His wife, Gaudairenca, was a poetess, and Paul Heyse has made her the central figure of one of his charming *Troubadour Novellen*. Raimon's poems betray no forebodings of the coming storm; when it broke, he lost his estate and fled to Raimon of Toulouse for shelter. The arrival of Pedro II. of Aragon at Toulouse in 1213 and his alliance with the Count of Toulouse cheered the troubadour's spirits : he thought there was a chance that he might recover his estate. He compliments Pedro on his determination in one poem and in another tells his lady, " the king has promised me that in a short time, I shall have Miraval again and my Audiart shall recover his Beaucaire ; then ladies and their lovers will regain their lost delights." Such was the attitude of many troubadours towards the crusade and they seem to represent the views of a certain section of society. There is no trace on this side of any sense of patriotism ; they hated the crusade because it destroyed the comforts of their happy existence. But the South of France had never as a whole acquired any real sense of nationalism : there was consequently no attempt at general or organised resistance and no leader to inspire such attempts was forth-coming.

On the other hand, special districts such as Toulouse, showed real courage and devotion. The crusaders often found much difficulty in maintaining a force adequate to conduct their operations after the first energy of the invasion had spent itself, and had the Count of Toulouse been an energetic and vigorous character, he might have been able to reverse the ultimate issue of the crusade. But, like many other petty lords his chief desire was to be left alone and he was at heart as little interested in the claims of Rome as in the attractions of heresy. His townspeople thought otherwise and the latter half of the *Chanson de la Croisade* reflects their hopes and fears and describes their struggles with a sympathy that often reaches the height of epic splendour. Similarly, certain troubadours were by no means absorbed in the practice of their art or the pursuit of their intrigues. Bernard Sicart de Marvejols has left us a vigorous satire against the crusaders who came for plunder and the clergy who drove them on. The greatest poet of this calamitous time is Peire Cardenal. His work falls within the years 1210 and 1230. The short notice that we have of him says that he belonged to Puy Notre Dame in Velay, that he was the son of a noble and was intended for an ecclesiastical career :

when he was of age, he was attracted by the pleasures of the world, became a troubadour and went from court to court, accompanied by a *joglar* : he was especially favoured by King Jaime I. of Aragon and died at the age of nearly a hundred years. He was no singer of love and the three of his *chansos* that remain are inspired by the misogyny that we have noted in the case of Marcabrun. Peire Cardenal's strength lay in the moral *sirventes* : he was a fiery soul, aroused to wrath by the sight of injustice and immorality and the special objects of his animosity are the Roman Catholic clergy and the high nobles. " The clergy call themselves shepherds and are murderers under a show of saintliness : when I look upon their dress I remember Isengrin (the wolf in the romance of Reynard, the Fox) who wished one day to break into the sheep-fold : but for fear of the dogs he dressed himself in a sheep-skin and then devoured as many as he would. Kings and emperors, dukes, counts and knights used to rule the world ;. now the priests have the power which they have gained by robbery and treachery, by hypocrisy, force and preaching." " Eagles and vultures smell not the carrion so readily as priests and preachers smell out the rich : a rich man is their friend and should a sickness strike him down, he must make them presents to the loss of his relations. Frenchmen and priests are reputed bad

and rightly so : usurers and traitors possess the
whole world, for with deceit have they so con-
founded the world that there is no class to whom
their doctrine is unknown." Peire inveighs against
the disgraces of particular orders ; the Preaching
Friars or Jacobin monks who discuss the relative
merits of special wines after their feasts, whose
lives are spent in disputes and who declare all who
differ from them to be Vaudois heretics, who worm
men's private affairs out of them, that they may
make themselves feared : some of his charges
against the monastic orders are quite unprintable.

No less vigorous are his invectives against the
rich and the social evils of his time. The tone of
regret that underlies Guiraut de Bornelh's satires
in this theme is replaced in Peire Cardenal's *sirventes*
by a burning sense of injustice. Covetousness,
the love of pleasure, injustice to the poor, treachery
and deceit and moral laxity are among his favourite
themes. " He who abhors truth and hates the
right, careers to hell and directs his course to the
abyss : for many a man builds walls and palaces
with the goods of others and yet the witless world
says that he is on the right path, because he is clever
and prosperous. As silver is refined in the fire, so
the patient poor are purified under grievous op-
pression : and with what splendour the shameless
rich man may feed and clothe himself, his riches

bring him nought but pain, grief and vexation of
spirit. But that affrights him not : capons and
game, good wine and the dainties of the earth con-
sole him and cheer his heart. Then he prays to
God and says ' I am poor and in misery.' Were
God to answer him He would say, ' thou liest ! ' ' "
To illustrate the degeneracy of the age, Peire relates
a fable, perhaps the only instance of this literary
form among the troubadours, upon the theme that
if all the world were mad, the one sane man would
be in a lunatic asylum : " there was a certain town,
I know not where, upon which a rain fell of such a
nature that all the inhabitants upon whom it fell,
lost their reason. All lost their reason except
one, who escaped because he was asleep in his house
when the rain came. When he awoke, he rose :
the rain had ceased, and he went out among the
people who were all committing follies. One was
clothed, another naked, another was spitting at
the sky : some were throwing sticks and stones,
tearing their coats, striking and pushing. . . .
The sane man was deeply surprised and saw that
they were mad ; nor could he find a single man in
his senses. Yet greater was their surprise at him,
and as they saw that he did not follow their example,
they concluded that he had lost his senses. . . . .
So one strikes him in front, another behind ; he is
dashed to the ground and trampled under foot. . . .

at length he flees to his house covered with mud, bruised and half dead and thankful for his escape " : The mad town, says Peire Cardenal, is the present world : the highest form of intelligence is the love and fear of God, but this has been replaced by greed, pride and malice ; consequently the " sense of God " seems madness to the world and he who refuses to follow the " sense of the world " is treated as a madman.

Peire Cardenal is thus by temperament a moral preacher ; he is not merely critical of errors, but has also a positive faith to propound. He is not an opponent of the papacy as an institution : the confession of faith which he utters in one of his *sirventes* shows that he would have been perfectly satisfied with the Roman ecclesiastical and doctrinal system, had it been properly worked. In this respect he differs from a contemporary troubadour, Guillem Figueira, whose violent satire against Rome shows him as opposed to the whole system from the papacy downwards. He was a native of Toulouse and migrated to Lombardy and to the court of Frederick II. when the crusade drove him from his home. " I wonder not, Rome, that men go astray, for thou hast cast the world into strife and misery ; virtue and good works die and are buried because of thee, treacherous Rome, thou guiding-star, thou root and branch of all iniquity

. . . Greed blindeth thy eyes, and too close dost
thou shear thy sheep . . . thou forgivest sins for
money, thou loadest thyself with a shameful burden.
Rome, we know of a truth that with the bait of
false forgiveness, thou hast snared in misery the
nobility of France, the people of Paris and the
noble King Louis (VIII., who died in the course of
the Albigeois crusade) ; thou didst bring him to
his death, for thy false preaching enticed him from
his land. Rome, thou has the outward semblance
of a lamb, so innocent is thy countenance, but within
thou are a ravening wolf, a crowned snake begotten
of a viper and therefore the devil greeteth thee as
the friend of his bosom." This sirventes was
answered by a *trobairitz*, Germonde of Montpelier,
but her reply lacks the vigour and eloquence of the
attack.

It is not to be supposed that the troubadours
turned to religious poetry simply because the
Albigeois crusade had raised the religious question.
Purely devotional poetry is found at an earlier
period.[29] It appears at first only sporadically,
and some of the greatest troubadours have left no
religious poems that have reached us. The fact
is, that the nature of troubadour poetry and its
homage to the married woman were incompatible
with the highest standard of religious devotion.
The famous *alba* of Guiraut de Bornelh invokes the

"glorious king, true light and splendour, Lord Almighty," for the purpose of praying that the lovers for whom the speaker is keeping watch may be undisturbed in interchange of their affections. Prayer for the success of attempted adultery is a contradiction in terms. For a theory of religion which could regard the Deity as a possible accomplice in crime, the Church of Southern France in the twelfth century is to blame : we cannot expect that the troubadours in general should be more religious than the professional exponents of religion. On the other hand, poems of real devotional feeling are found, even from the earliest times : the sensual Count of Poitiers, the first troubadour known to us, concludes his career with a poem of resignation bidding farewell to the world, "leaving all that I love, the brilliant life of chivalry, but since it pleases God, I resign myself and pray Him to keep me among His own." Many troubadours, as has been said, ended their lives in monasteries and the disappointments or griefs which drove them to this course often aroused religious feelings, regrets for past follies and resolutions of repentance, which found expression in poetry. Peire d'Auvergne wrote several religious hymns after his retirement from the world ; these are largely composed of reiterated articles of the Christian faith in metrical form and are as unpoetical as they are orthodox.

Crusade poems and *planhs* upon the deaths of famous nobles or patrons are religious only in a secondary sense. A fine religious *alba* is ascribed to Folquet of Marseilles—

> Vers Dieus, e·l vostre nom e de sancta Maria
> m'esvelherai hueimais, pus l'estela del dia
> ven daus Jerusalem que' m'ensenha qu'ieu dia :
> estatz sus e levatz,
> senhor, que Dieu amatz !
> que·l jorns es aprosmatz
> e la nuech ten sa via ;
> e sia·n Dieus lauzatz
> per nos e adoratz,
> e·l preguem que·ns don patz
> a tota nostra via.
> La nuech vai e·l jorns ve
> ab clar cel e sere,
> e l'alba no·s rete
> ans ven belh' e complia.

"True God, in Thy name and in the name of Saint Mary will I awake henceforth, since the star of day rises from o'er Jerusalem, bidding me say, ' Up and arise, sirs, who love God ! For the day is nigh, and the night departs ; and let God be praised and adored by us and let us pray Him that He give us peace for all our lives. Night goes and day comes with clear serene sky, and the dawn delays not but comes fair and perfect.'"

At the close of the Albigeois crusade the Virgin Mary becomes the theme of an increasing number of lyric poems. These are not like the farewells to the world, uttered by weary troubadours, and dictated by individual circumstances, but are inspired by an increase of religious feeling in the public to whom the troubadours appealed. Peire Cardenal began the series and a similar poem is attributed to Perdigon, a troubadour who joined the crusaders and fought against his old patrons; though the poem is probably not his, it belongs to a time but little posterior to the crusade. The cult of the Virgin had obvious attractions as a subject for troubadours whose profane songs would not have been countenanced by St Dominic and his preachers and religious poetry dealing with the subject could easily borrow not only the metrical forms but also many technical expressions which troubadours had used in singing of worldly love. They could be the servants of a heavenly mistress and attribute to her all the graces and beauty of form and character. It has been supposed that the Virgin was the mysterious love sung by Jaufre Rudel and the supposition is not inconsistent with the language of his poems. Guiraut Riquier, the last of the troubadours, provides examples of this new *genre* : from the fourteenth century it was the only kind of poem admitted by the school of Toulouse and the Jeux Floraux crowned many poems of this nature. These, however, have little in common with classical troubadour poetry except language. The following stanzas from the well-known hymn to the Virgin by Peire de Corbiac, will give an idea of the character of this poetry.

> Domna, rosa ses espina,
> sobre totas flors olens,
> verga seca frug fazens,
> terra que ses labor grana,
> estela, del solelh maire,
> noirissa del vostre paire,
> el mon nulha no·us semelha
> ni londana ni vezina.
>
> Domna, verge pura e fina,
> ans que fos l'enfantamens,
> et apres tot eissamens,
> receup en vos carn humana
> Jesu Crist, nostre salvaire,
> si com ses trencamen faire
> intra·l bels rais, quan solelha,
> per la fenestra veirina.
>
> Domna, estela marina
> de las autras plus luzens,
> la mars nos combat e·l vens ;
> mostra nos via certana ;
> car si·ns vols a bon port traire
> non tem nau ni governaire
> ni tempest que·ns destorbelha
> ni·l sobern de la marina.

"Lady, rose without thorn, sweet above all flowers, dry rod bearing fruit, earth bringing forth fruit without toil, star, mother of the sun, nurse of thine own Father, in the world no woman is like to thee, neither far nor near.

Lady, virgin pure and fair before the birth was and afterwards the same, Jesus Christ our Saviour received human flesh in thee, just as without causing flaw, the fair ray enters through the window-pane when the sun shines.

Lady, star of the sea, brighter than the other stars, the sea and the wind buffet us; show thou us the right way: for if thou wilt bring us to a fair haven, ship nor helmsman fears not tempest nor tide lest it trouble us."

CHAPTER VII

THE TROUBADOURS IN ITALY

To study the development of troubadour literature only in the country of its origin would be to gain a very incomplete idea of its influence. The movement, as we have already said, crossed the Pyrenees, the Alps and the Rhine, and Italy at least owed the very existence of its lyric poetry to the impulse first given by the troubadours. Close relations between Southern France and Northern Italy had existed from an early period : commercial intercourse between the towns on the Mediterranean was in some cases strengthened by treaties ; the local nobles were connected by feudal ties resulting from the suzerainty of the Holy Roman Empire. Hence it was natural for troubadours and *joglars* to visit the Italian towns. Their own language was not so remote from the Italian dialects as to raise any great obstacle to the circulation of their poetry and the petty princes of Northern Italy lent as ready an ear to troubadour songs as the local lords in the South of France. Peire Vidal was at the court of the Marquis of Montferrat so early as 1195 ; the Marquis of Este, the Count of

San Bonifacio at Verona, the Count of Savoy at
Turin, the Emperor Frederick II. and other lords
of less importance offered a welcome to Provençal
poets. More than twenty troubadours are thus
known to have visited Italy and in some cases to
have made a stay of considerable length. The
result was that their poetry soon attracted Italian
disciples and imitators. Provençal became the
literary language of the noble classes and an Italian
school of troubadours arose, of whom Sordello is
the most remarkable figure.

Raimbaut de Vaqueiras, who spent a considerable part of his career (1180–1207) with the Marquis
of Montferrat, belongs as a troubadour quite as
much to Italy as to Southern France. He was
the son of a poor noble of Orange and became
a troubadour at the court of William IV. of
Orange ; he exchanged *tensos* with his patron with
whom he seems to have been on very friendly
terms and to whom he refers by the pseudonym
Engles (English), the reason for which is as yet
unknown. Some time later than 1189, he left the
court of Orange, apparently in consequence of a
dispute with his patron and made his way to Italy,
where he led a wandering life until he was admitted
to the court of the Marquis of Montferrat. To this
period of his career belongs the well-known poem
in which he pays his addresses to a Genoese lady.

" Lady, I have prayed you long to love me of your kindliness . . . my heart is more drawn to you than to any lady of Genoa. I shall be well rewarded if you will love me and shall be better recompensed for my trouble than if Genoa belonged to me with all the wealth that is there heaped up." The lady then replies in her own Genoese dialect : she knows nothing of the conventions of courtly love, and informs the troubadour that her husband is a better man than he and that she will have nothing to do with him. The poem is nothing but a *jeu d'esprit* based upon the contrast between troubadour sentiments and the honest but unpoetical views of the middle class ; it is interesting to philologists as containing one of the earliest known specimens of Italian dialect. An example of the Tuscan dialect is also found in the *descort* by Raimbaut. This is a poem in irregular metre, intended to show the perturbation of the poet's mind. Raimbaut increased this effect by writing in five different languages. He found a ready welcome from Bonifacio II. at the court of Montferrat which Peire Vidal also visited. The marquis dubbed him knight and made him his brother in arms. Raimbaut fell in love with Beatrice, the sister of the marquis, an intimacy which proceeded upon the regular lines of courtly love. He soon found an opportunity of showing his devotion to the

G

marquis. In 1194 Henry VI. made an expedition to Sicily to secure the claims of his wife, Constance, to that kingdom : the Marquis Boniface as a vassal of the imperial house followed the Emperor and Raimbaut accompanied his contingent. He refers to his share in the campaign in a later letter to the marquis.[30]

> Et ai per vos estat en greu preyzo
> Per vostra guerra e n'ai a vostre pro
> Fag maynt assaut et ars maynta maiso
> Et a Messina vos cobri del blizo ;
> En la batalha vos vinc en tal sazo
> Que·us ferion pel pietz e pel mento
> Dartz e cairels, sagetas e trenso.

"For your sake I have been in hard captivity in your war, and to do you service I have made many an assault and burned many a house. At Messina I covered you with the shield ; I came to you in the battle at the moment when they hurled at your breast and chin darts and quarrels, arrows and lance-shafts." The captivity was endured in the course of the marquis's wars in Italy, and the troubadour refers to a seafight between the forces of Genoa and Pisa in the Sicilian campaign. In 1202 he followed his master upon the crusade which practically ended at Constantinople. He had composed a vigorous *sirventes* urging Christian men to join the movement, but he does not himself show any great enthusiasm to take the cross. " I would rather, if it please you, die in that land than live and remain here. For us God was raised upon the cross, received death, suffered the passion, was scourged and loaded with chains and crowned with thorns upon the cross . . . . Fair Cavalier (*i.e.* Beatrice) I know not whether I shall stay for your sake or take the cross ; I know not whether I shall go or remain, for I die with grief if I see you and I am like to die if I am far from you." So also in the letter quoted above.

> E cant anetz per crozar a Saysso,
> Ieu non avia cor—Dieus m'o perdo—
> Que passes mar, mas per vostre resso
> Levey la crotz e pris confessio.

" And when you went to Soissons to take the cross, I did not intend—may God forgive me—to cross the sea, but to increase your fame I took the cross and made confession." The count lost his life, as Villehardouin relates, in a skirmish with the Bulgarians in 1207. Raimbaut de Vaqueiras probably fell at the same time.

This is enough to show that troubadours who came to Italy could make the country a second home, and find as much occupation in love, war and politics as they had ever found in Southern France. Aimeric de Pegulhan, Gaucelm Faidit,

Uc de Saint-Circ,[31] the author of some troubadour biographies, were among the best known of those who visited Italy. The last named is known to have visited Pisa and another troubadour of minor importance, Guillem de la Tor, was in Florence. Thus the visits of the troubadours were by no means confined to the north.

It was, therefore, natural that Italians should imitate the troubadours whose art proved so successful at Italian courts and some thirty Italian troubadours are known to us. Count Manfred II. and Albert, the Marquis of Malaspina, engaged in *tensos* with Peire Vidal and Raimbaut de Vaqueiras respectively and are the first Italians known to have written in Provençal. Genoa produced a number of Italian troubadours of whom the best were Lanfranc Cigala and Bonifacio Calvo. The latter was a wanderer and spent some time in Castile at the court of Alfonso X. Lanfranc Cigala was a judge in his native town : from him survive a *sirventes* against Bonifacio III. of Montferrat who had abandoned the cause of Frederick II., crusade poems and a *sirventes* against the obscure style. The Venetian Bartolomeo Zorzi was a prisoner at Genoa from 1266 to 1273, having been captured by the Genoese. The troubadour of Genoa, Bonifacio Calvo, had written a vigorous invective against Venice, to which the captive troubadour composed

an equally strong reply addressed to Bonifacio
Calvo ; the latter sought him out and the two
troubadours became friends. The most famous,
however, of the Italian troubadours is certainly
Sordello.

There is much uncertainty concerning the facts
of Sordello's life ; he was born at Goito, near Mantua,
and was of noble family. His name is not to be
derived from *sordidus*, but from *Surdus*, a not
uncommon patronymic in North Italy during the
thirteenth century. Of his early years nothing
is known : at some period of his youth he entered
the court of Count Ricciardo di san Bonifazio, the
lord of Verona, where he fell in love with his
master's wife, Cunizza da Romano (Dante, *Par*. ix.
32), and eloped with her. The details of this affair
are entirely obscure ; according to some com-
mentators, it was the final outcome of a family feud,
while others assert that the elopement took place
with the connivance of Cunizza's brother, the
notorious Ezzelino III. (*Inf*. xii. 110) : the date
is approximately 1225. At any rate, Sordello and
Cunizza betook themselves to Ezzelino's court.
Then, according to the Provençal biography, follows
his secret marriage with Otta, and his flight from
Treviso, to escape the vengeance of her angry
relatives. He thus left Italy about the year 1229,
and retired to the South of France, where he

visited the courts of Provence, Toulouse, Roussillon,
penetrating also into Castile. A chief authority
for these wanderings is the troubadour Peire Bremon
Ricas Novas, whose *sirventes* speaks of him as being
in Spain at the court of the king of Leon : this was
Alfonso IX., who died in the year 1230. He also
visited Portugal, but for this no date can be assigned.
Allusions in his poems show that he was in Provence
before 1235 : about ten years later we find him
at the court of the Countess Beatrice (*Par.* vi. 133),
daughter of Raimon Berengar, Count of Provence,
and wife of Charles 1. of Anjou. Beatrice may
have been the subject of several of his love poems :
but the " senhal " Restaur and Agradiva, which
conceal the names possibly of more than one lady
cannot be identified. From 1252-1265 his name
appears in several Angevin treaties and records,
coupled with the names of other well-known nobles,
and he would appear to have held a high place in
Charles' esteem. It is uncertain whether he took
part in the first crusade of St Louis, in 1248-1251,
at which Charles was present : but he followed
Charles on his Italian expedition against Manfred
in 1265, and seems to have been captured by the
Ghibellines before reaching Naples. At any rate,
he was a prisoner at Novara in September 1266 ;
Pope Clement IV. induced Charles to ransom him,
and in 1269, as a recompense for his services, he

received five castles in the Abruzzi, near the river Pescara : shortly afterwards he died. The circumstances of his death are unknown, but from the fact that he is placed by Dante among those who were cut off before they could repent it has been conjectured that he came to a violent end.

Sordello's restless life and his intrigues could be exemplified from the history of many another troubadour and neither his career nor his poetry, which with two exceptions, is of no special originality, seems to justify the portrait drawn of him by Dante ; while Browning's famous poem has nothing in common with the troubadour except the name. These exceptions, however, are notable. The first is a *sirventes* composed by Sordello on the death of his patron Blacatz in 1237. He invites to the funeral feast the Roman emperor, Frederick II., the kings of France, England and Aragon, the counts of Champagne, Toulouse and Provence. They are urged to eat of the dead man's heart, that they may gain some tincture of his courage and nobility. Each is invited in a separate stanza in which the poet reprehends the failings of the several potentates.

> Del rey engles me platz, quar es pauc coratjos,
> Que manje pro del cor, pueys er valens e bos,
> E cobrara la terra, per que viu de pretz blos,
> Que·l tol lo reys de Fransa, quar lo sap nualhos ;

E lo reys castelas tanh qu'en manje per dos,
Quar dos regismes ten, e per l'un non es pros ;
Mas, s'elh en vol manjar, tanh qu'en manj'a rescos,
Que, si·l mair'o sabra, batria·l ab bastos.

" As concerns the English King (Henry III.) it pleases me, for he is little courageous, that he should eat well of the heart ; then he will be valiant and good and will recover the land (for loss of which he lives bereft of worth), which the King of France took from him, for he knows him to be of no account. And the King of Castile (Ferdinand III. of Castile and Leon), it is fitting that he eat of it for two, for he holds two realms and he is not sufficient for one ; but if he will eat of it, 'twere well that he eat in secret : for if his mother were to know it, she would beat him with staves."

This idea, which is a commonplace in the folk-lore of many countries, attracted attention. Two contemporary troubadours attempted to improve upon it. Bertran d'Alamanon said that the heart should not be divided among the cowards, enumerated by Sordello, but given to the noble ladies of the age : Peire Bremon proposed a division of the body. The point is that Dante in the Purgatorio represents Sordello as showing to Virgil the souls of those who, while singing *Salve Regina*, ask to be pardoned for their neglect of duty and among them appear the rulers whom Sordello had satirised in his *sirventes*. Hence it seems that it was this composition which attracted Dante's attention to Sordello. The other important poem is the *Ensenhamen*, a didactic work of instruction upon the manner and conduct proper to a courtier and a lover. Here, and also in some of his lyric poems, Sordello represents the transition to a new idea of love which was more fully developed by the school of Guido Guinicelli and found its highest expression in Dante's lyrics and Vita Nuova. Love is now rather a mystical idea than a direct affection for a particular lady : the lover is swayed by a spiritual and intellectual ideal, and the motive of physical attraction recedes to the background. The cause of love, however, remains unchanged : love enters through the eyes ; sight is delight.

We must now turn southwards. A school of poetry had grown up in Sicily at the court of Frederick II. No doubt he favoured those troubadours whose animosity to the papacy had been aroused by the Albigeois crusade : such invective as that which Guillem Figueira could pour forth would be useful to him in his struggle against the popes. But the emperor was himself a man of unusual culture, with a keen interest in literary and scientific pursuits : he founded a university at Naples, collected manuscripts and did much to make Arabic learning known to the West. He was a poet and the importance of the Sicilian school consists in the fact that while the subject matter of their songs was lifted from troubadour poetry, the language which they used belonged to the Italian peninsula. The dialect of these *provenzaleggianti* was not pure Sicilian but was probably a literary language containing elements drawn from other dialects, as happened long before in the case of the troubadours themselves. The best known representatives of this school, Pier delle Vigne, Jacopo da Lentini and Guido delle Colonne are familiar to students of Dante. After their time no one questioned the fact that lyric poetry written in Italian was a possible achievement.

The influence of the Sicilian school extended to Central Italy and Tuscany; Dante tells us that all Italian poetry preceding his own age was known as Sicilian. The early Tuscan poets were, mediately or immediately, strongly influenced by Provençal. The first examples of the sonnet, by Dante da Majano, were written in that language. But such poetry was little more than a rhetorical exercise. It was the revival of learning and the Universities, in particular that of Bologna, which inspired the *dolce stil nuovo*, of which the first exponent was Guido Giunicelli. Love was now treated from a philosophical point of view : hitherto, the Provençal school had maintained the thesis that " sight is delight," that love originated from seeing and pleasing, penetrated to the heart and occupied the thoughts, after passing through the eyes. So Aimeric de Pegulhan

> Perque tuit li fin aman
> Sapchan qu'amors es fina bevolenza
> Que nais del cor e dels huelh, ses duptar.

" Wherefore let all pure lovers know that love is pure unselfishness which is born undoubtedly from the heart and from the eyes," a sentiment thus repeated by Guido delle Colonne of the Sicilian school.

> Dal cor si move un spirito in vedere
> D'in ochi'n ochi, di femina e d'omo
> Per lo quel si concria uno piacere.

The philosophical school entirely transformed this conception. Love seeks the noble heart by affinity, as the bird seeks the tree : the noble heart cannot but love, and love inflames and purifies its nobility, as the power of the Deity is transmitted to the heavenly beings. When this idea had been once evolved, Provençal poetry could no longer be a moving force ; it was studied but was not imitated. Its influence had lasted some 150 years, and as far as Italy is concerned it was Arabic learning, Aristotle and Thomas Aquinas who slew the troubadours more certainly than Simon de Montfort and his crusaders. The day of superficial prettiness and of the cult of form had passed ; love conjoined with learning, a desire to pierce to the roots of things, a greater depth of thought and earnestness were the characteristics of the new school.

Dante's debt to the troubadours, with whose literature he was well acquainted, is therefore the debt of Italian literature as a whole. Had not the troubadours developed their theory of courtly love, with its influence upon human nature, we cannot say what course early Italian literature might have run. Moreover, the troubadours provided Italy and other countries also with perfect models of poetical form. The sonnet, the terza rima and any other form used by Dante are of Provençal origin. And what is true of Dante and his Beatrice is no less true of Petrarch and his Laura and of many another who may be sought in histories specially devoted to this subject.

CHAPTER VIII

THE TROUBADOURS IN SPAIN

THE South of France had been connected with the
North of Spain from a period long antecedent to
the first appearance of troubadour poetry. As
early as the Visigoth period, Catalonia had been
united to Southern France ; in the case of this
province the tie was further strengthened by com-
munity of language. On the western side of the
Pyrenees a steady stream of pilgrims entered the
Spanish peninsula on their way to the shrine of St
James of Compostella in Galicia ; this road was,
indeed, known in Spain as the " French road."
Catalonia was again united with Provence by the
marriage of Raimon Berengar III. with a Provençal
heiress in 1112. As the counts of Barcelona and
the kings of Aragon held possessions in Southern
France, communications between the two countries
were naturally frequent.

We have already had occasion to refer to the
visits of various troubadours to the courts of Spain.
The " reconquista," the reconquest of Spain from
the Moors, was in progress during the twelfth and
thirteenth centuries, and various crusade poems

were written by troubadours summoning help to
the Spaniards in their struggles. Marcabrun was
the author of one of the earliest of these, composed
for the benefit of Alfonso VIII. of Castile and possibly
referring to his expedition against the Moors in
1147, which was undertaken in conjunction with
the kings of Navarre and Aragon. The poem is
interesting for its repetition of the word *lavador* or
piscina, used as an emblem of the crusade in which
the participants would be cleansed of their sins.[32]

> Pax in nomine Domini !
> Fetz Marcabrus los motz e·l so.
> 　　Aujatz que di :
> Cum nos a fait per sa doussor,
> Lo Seignorius celestiaus
> Probet de nos un lavador
> C'anc, fors outramar, no·n' fon taus,
> En de lai deves Josaphas :
> E d'aquest de sai vos conort.

" Pax, etc.,—Marcabrun composed the words and
the air. Hear what he says. How, by his goodness, the Lord of Heaven, has made near us a piscina,
such as there never was, except beyond the sea,
there by Josaphat, and for this one near here do
I exhort you."

Alfonso II. of Aragon (1162-1196) was a constant
patron of the troubadours, and himself an exponent
of their art. He belonged to the family of the

counts of Barcelona which became in his time one
of the most powerful royal houses in the West of
Europe. He was the grandson of Raimon Berengar
III. and united to Barcelona by marriage and
diplomacy, the kingdom of Aragon, Provence and
Roussillon. His continual visits to the French
part of his dominions gave every opportunity to
the troubadours to gain his favour : several were
continually about him and there were few who
did not praise his liberality. A discordant note
is raised by Bertran de Born, who composed some
violent *sirventes* against Alfonso ; he was actuated
by political motives : Alfonso had joined the King
of England in his operations against Raimon V. of
Toulouse and Bertran's other allies and had been
present at the capture of Bertran's castle of Hautefort in 1183. The biography relates that in the
course of the siege, the King of Aragon, who had
formerly been in friendly relations with Bertran,
sent a messenger into the fortress asking for pro-
visions. These Bertran supplied with the request
that the king would secure the removal of the siege
engines from a particular piece of wall, which was
on the point of destruction and would keep the
information secret. Alfonso, however, betrayed
the message and the fortress was captured. The
razo further relates the touching scene to
which we have already referred when Bertran

moved Henry II. to clemency by a reference to the death of the "young king." The account of Alfonso's supposed treachery is probably no less unhistorical : the siege lasted only a week and it is unlikely that the besiegers would have been reduced to want in so short a time. It was probably invented to explain the hostility on Bertran's part which dated from the wars between Alfonso and Raimon V. of Toulouse. This animosity was trumpeted forth in two lampooning *sirventes* criticising the public policy and the private life of the Spanish King. His accusations of meanness and trickery seem to be based on nothing more reliable than current gossip.

Peire Vidal, with the majority of the troubadours, shows himself a vigorous supporter of Alfonso. Referring to this same expedition of 1183 he asserted " Had I but a speedy horse, the king might sleep in peace at Balaguer : I would keep Provence and Montpelier in such order that robbers and freebooters should no longer plunder Venaissin and Crau. When I have put on my shining cuirass and girded on the sword that Guigo lately gave me, the earth trembles beneath my feet ; no enemy so mighty who does not forthwith avoid out of my path, so great is their fear of me when they hear my steps." These boasts in the style of Captain Matamoros are, of course, not serious : the poet's personal appearance seems to have been enough to preclude any suppositions of the kind. In another poem he sings the praises of Sancha, daughter of Alfonso VIII. of Castile, who married Alfonso II. of Aragon in 1174. With the common sense in political matters which is so strangely conjoined with the whimsicality of his actions, he puts his finger upon the weak spot in Spanish politics when he refers to the disunion between the four kings, Alfonso II. of Aragon, Alfonso IX. of Leon, Alfonso VIII. of Castile and Sancho Garcés of Navarre : " little honour is due to the four kings of Spain for that they cannot keep peace with one another ; since in other respects they are of great worth, dexterous, open, courteous and loyal, so that they should direct their efforts to better purpose and wage war elsewhere against the people who do not believe our law, until the whole of Spain professes one and the same faith."

The Monk of Montaudon, Peire Raimon of Toulouse, Uc de San Circ, Uc Brunet and other troubadours of less importance also enjoyed Alfonso's patronage. Guiraut de Bornelh sent a poem to the Catalonian court in terms which seemed to show that the simple style of poetry was there preferred to complicated obscurities. The same troubadour was sufficiently familiar with Alfonso's successor, Pedro II., to take part in a *tenso* with him.

H

Pedro II. (1196-1213) was no less popular with the troubadours than his father. Aimeric de Pegulhan, though more closely connected with the court of Castile, is loud in his praises of Pedro, " the flower of courtesy, the green leaf of delight, the fruit of noble deeds." Pedro supported his brother-in-law, Raimon VI. of Toulouse, against the crusaders and Simon de Montfort during the Albigeois crusade and was killed near Toulouse in the battle of Muret. The Chanson de la Croisade does not underestimate the impression made by his death.

> Mot fo grans lo dampnatges e·l dols e·l perdementz
> Cant lo reis d'Arago remas mort e sagnens,
> E mot d'autres baros, don fo grans l'aunimens
> A tot crestianesme et a trastotas gens.

" Great was the damage and the grief and the loss when the King of Aragon remained dead and bleeding with many other barons, whence was great shame to all Christendom and to all people."

The Court of Castile attracted the attention and the visits of the troubadours, chiefly during the reign of Alfonso VIII. (or III.; 1158-1214) the hero of Las Navas de Tolosa, the most decisive defeat which the Arab power in the West had sustained since the days of Charles Martel. The preceding defeat of Alfonso's forces at Alarcos in 1195 had called forth a fine crusade *sirventes* from Folquet of Marseilles appealing to Christians in general

and the King of Aragon in particular to join forces
against the infidels. The death of Alfonso's son,
Fernando, in 1211 from an illness contracted in
the course of a campaign against the infidels was
lamented by Guiraut de Calanso, a Gascon troubadour,

> Lo larc e·l franc, lo valen e·l grazitz,
> Don cuiavon qu'en fos esmendatz
> Lo jove reys, e·n Richartz lo prezatz
> E·l coms Jaufres, tug li trey valen fraire.

" The generous and frank, the worthy and attractive of whom men thought that in him were increased the qualities of the young king, of Richard
the high renowned, and of the Count Godfrey, all
the three valiant brothers." Peire Vidal in one of
the poems which he addressed to Alfonso VIII.,
speaks of the attractions of Spain. " Spain is a
good country ; its kings and lords are kindly and
loving, generous and noble, of courteous company ;
other barons there are, noble and hospitable, men
of sense and knowledge, valiant and renowned."
Raimon Vidal of Bezaudun, a Catalonian troubadour
has given a description of Alfonso's court in one of
his *novelas*. " I wish to relate a story which I
heard a joglar tell at the court of the wisest king
that ever was, King Alfonso of Castile, where were
presents and gifts, judgment, worth and courtesy,
spirit and chivalry, though he was not anointed

or sacred, but crowned with praise, sense, worth and prowess. The king gathered many knights to his court, many *joglars* and rich barons and when the court was filled Queen Eleanor came in dressed so that no one saw her body. She came wrapped closely in a cloak of silken fabric fine and fair called sisclaton ; it was red with a border of silver and had a golden lion broidered on it. She bowed to the king and took her seat on one side at some distance. Then, behold, a *joglar* come before the king, frank and debonair, who said ' King, noble emperor, I have come to you thus and I pray you of your goodness that my tale may be heard.' " The scene concludes, " Joglar, I hold the story which you have related as good, amusing and fair and you also the teller of it and I will order such reward to be given to you that you shall know that the story has indeed pleased me."

The crown of Castile was united with that of Leon by Fernando III. (1230-1262) the son of Alfonso IX. of Leon. Lanfranc Cigala, the troubadour of Genoa, excuses the Spaniards at this time for their abstention from the Crusades to Jerusalem on the ground that they were fully occupied in their struggles with the Moors. Fernando is one of the kings to whom Sordello refers in the famous *sirventes* of the divided heart, as also is Jaime I. of Aragon (1213-1276), the " Conquistador," of whom much is

heard in the poetry of the troubadours. He was
born at Montpelier and was fond of revisiting his
birthplace ;   troubadours   whom   he   there   met
accompanied him to Spain, joined in his expeditions
and enjoyed his generosity.   His court became a
place of refuge for those who had been driven out
of Southern France by the Albigeois crusade ;
Peire Cardenal, Bernard Sicart de Marvejols and
N'At de Mons of Toulouse visited him.   His popu-
larity with the troubadours was considerably shaken
by his policy in 1242, when a final attempt was
made to throw off the yoke imposed upon Southern France as the result of the Albigeois crusade.
Isabella of Angoulême, the widow of John of
England, had married the Count de la Marche ;
she urged him to rise against the French and induced her son, Henry III. of England, to support
him.   Henry hoped to regain his hold of Poitou
and was further informed that the Count of Toulouse
and the Spanish kings would join the alliance.
There seems to have been a general belief that
Jaime would take the opportunity of avenging his
father's death at Muret.   However, no Spanish
help was forthcoming ;   the allies were defeated
at Saintes and at Taillebourg and this abortive
rising ended in 1243.   Guillem de Montanhagol
says in a *sirventes* upon this event, " If King Jaime,
with whom we have never broken faith, had kept

the agreement which is said to have been made between him and us, the French would certainly have had cause to grieve and lament." Bernard de Rovenhac shows greater bitterness : " the king of Aragon is undoubtedly well named Jacme (jac from jazer, to lie down) for he is too fond of lying down and when anyone despoils him of his land, he is so feeble that he does not offer the least opposition." Bernard Sicart de Marvejols voices the grief of his class at the failure of the rising : " In the day I am full of wrath and in the night I sigh betwixt sleeping and waking ; wherever I turn, I hear the courteous people crying humbly ' Sire ' to the French." These outbursts do not seem to have roused Jaime to any great animosity against the troubadour class. Aimeric de Belenoi belauds him, Peire Cardenal is said to have enjoyed his favour, and other minor troubadours refer to him in flattering terms.

The greatest Spanish patron of the troubadours was undoubtedly Alfonso X. of Castile (1254-1284). El Sabio earned his title by reason of his enlightened interest in matters intellectual ; he was himself a poet, procured the translation of many scientific books and provided Castile with a famous code of laws. The Italian troubadours Bonifaci Calvo and Bartolomeo Zorzi were welcomed to his court, to which many others came from Provence. One of his favourites was the troubadour who was the last representative of the old school, Guiraut Riquier of Narbonne. He was born between 1230 and 1235, when the Albigeois crusade was practically over and when troubadour poetry was dying, as much from its own inherent lack of vitality as from the change of social and political environment which the upheaval of the previous twenty years had produced. Guiraut Riquier applied to a Northern patron for protection, a proceeding unexampled in troubadour history and the patron he selected was the King of France himself. Neither Saint Louis nor his wife were in the least likely to provide a market for Guiraut's wares and the Paris of that day was by no means a centre of literary culture. The troubadour, therefore, tried his fortune with Alfonso X. whose liberality had become almost proverbial. There he seems to have remained for some years and to have been well content, in spite of occasional friction with other suitors for the king's favour. His description of Catalonia is interesting.

> Pus astres no m'es donatz
> Que de mi dons bes m'eschaia,
> Ni nulho nos plazers no·l platz,
> Ni ay poder que·m n'estraia,
> Ops m'es qu'ieu sia fondatz
> En via d'amor veraia,
> E puesc n'apenre assatz

En Cataluenha la gaia,
Entrels Catalas valens
E las donas avinens.

　　Quar dompneys, pretz e valors,
Joys e gratz e cortesia,
Sens e sabers et honors,
Bels parlars, bella paria,
E largueza et amors,
Conoyssensa e cundia,
Troban manten e socors
En Cataluenha a tria,
Entrels, etc.

"Since my star has not granted me that from my lady happiness should fall to me, since no pleasure that I can give pleases her and I have no power to forget her, I must needs enter upon the road of true love and I can learn it well enough in gay Catalonia among the Catalonians, men of worth, and their kindly ladies. For courtesy, worth, joy, gratitude and gallantry, sense, knowledge, honour, fair speech, fair company, liberality and love, learning and grace find maintenance and support in Catalonia entirely."

Between thirty and forty poets of Spanish extraction are known to have written Provençal poetry. Guillem de Tudela of Navarre wrote the first part of the *Chanson de la Croisade albigeoise*; Serveri de Gerona wrote didactic and devotional poetry, showing at least ingenuity of technique;

Amanieu des Escas has left love letters and didactic works for the instruction of young people in the rules of polite behaviour. But the influence of Provençal upon the native poetry of Spain proper was but small, in spite of the welcome which the troubadours found at the courts of Castile, Aragon, Leon and Navarre. Troubadour poetry required a peaceful and an aristocratic environment, and the former at least of these conditions was not provided by the later years of Alfonso X. Northern French influence was also strong : numerous French immigrants were able to settle in towns newly founded or taken from the Moors. The warlike and adventurous spirit of Northern and Central Spain preferred epic to lyric poetry : and the outcome was the *cantar de gesta* and the *romance*, the lyrico-narrative or ballad poem.

This was not the course of development followed either in the Eastern or Western coasts of the peninsula. Catalonia was as much a part of the Provençal district as of Spain. To the end of the thirteenth century Catalonian poets continued to write in the language of the troubadours, often breaking the strict rules of rime correspondence and of grammar, but refusing to use their native dialect. Religious poems of popular and native origin appear to have existed, but even the growth of a native prose was unable to overcome the preference for Provençal in the composition of lyrics. Guiraut de Cabreira is remembered for the 213 lines which he wrote to instruct his *joglar* Cabra ; Guiraut upbraids this performer for his ignorance, and details a long series of legends and poems which a competent *joglar* ought to know. Guiraut de Calanso wrote an imitation of this diatribe. The best known of the Catalonian troubadours is Raimon Vidal of Besadun, both for his *novelas* and also for his work on Provençal grammar and metre, *Las rasos de trobar*,[33] which was written for the benefit of his compatriots who desired to avoid solecisms or mistakes when composing. " Forasmuch as I, Raimon Vidal, have seen and known that few men know or have known the right manner of composing poetry (trobar) I desire to make this book that men may know and understand which of the troubadours have composed best and given the best instruction to those who wish to learn how they should follow the right manner of composing. . . . All Christian people, Jews, Saracens, emperors, princes, kings, dukes, counts, viscounts, vavassors and all other nobles with clergy, citizens and villeins, small and great, daily give their minds to composing and singing. . . . In this science of composing the troubadours are gone astray and I will tell you wherefore. The hearers who do not understand anything when they hear a fine poem will pretend that they understand perfectly . . . because they think that men would consider it a fault in them if they said that they did not understand. . . . And if when they hear a bad troubadour, they do understand, they will praise his singing because they understand it ; or if they will not praise, at least they will not blame him ; and thus the troubadours are deceived and the hearers are to blame for it." Raimon Vidal proceeds to say that the pure language is that of Provence or of Limousin or of Saintonge or Auvergne or Quercy : " wherefore I tell you, that when I use the term Limousin, I mean all those lands and those which border them or are between them." He was apparently the first to use the term Limousin to describe classical Provençal, and when it became applied to literary Catalonian, as distinguished from *plá Catalá*, the vulgar tongue, the result was some confusion. Provençal influence was more permanent in Catalonia than in any other part of Spain ; in 1393, the Consistorium of the *Gay saber* was founded in imitation of the similar association at Toulouse. Most of the troubadour poetical forms and the doctrines of the Toulouse *Leys d'Amors* were retained, until Italian influence began to oust Provençal towards the close of the fifteenth century.

On the western side of Spain, Provençal influence evoked a brief and brilliant literature in the Galician

or Portuguese school. Its most brilliant period was
the age of Alfonso X. of Castile, one of its most
illustrious exponents, and that of Denis of Portugal
(1280-1325). The dates generally accepted for
the duration of this literature are 1200-1385 ; it
has left to us some 2000 lyric poems, the work of
more than 150 poets, including four kings and a
number of nobles of high rank. French and Provençal culture had made its way gradually and by
various routes to the western side of the Spanish
peninsula.

We have already referred to the pilgrim route
to the shrine of Compostella, by which a steady
stream of foreign influence entered the country.
The same effect was produced by crusaders who
came to help the Spaniards in their struggle against
the Moors, and by foreign colonists who helped to
Christianise the territories conquered from the
Mohammedans. The capture of Lisbon in 1147
increased maritime intercourse with the North.
Individuals from Portugal also visited Northern
and Southern France, after the example of their
Spanish neighbours. References to Portugal in
the poetry of the troubadours are very scarce,
nor is there any definite evidence that any troubadour visited the country. This fact is in striking
contrast with the loud praises of the Spanish
courts. None the less, such visits must have

taken place : Sancho I. had French *jongleurs* in his pay during the twelfth century and the Portuguese element in the five-language *descort* of Raimbaut de Vaqueiras shows that communication between Provençal poets and Portuguese or Galician districts must have existed. The general silence of the troubadours may be due to the fact that communication began at a comparatively late period and was maintained between Portugal and Spanish courts, and not directly between Portugal and Southern France.

Alfonso X. of Castile himself wrote many poems in the Galician or Portuguese dialect ; perhaps his choice was dictated by reasons analogous to those which impelled Italian and Catalonian poets to write in Provençal. The general body of Portuguese poetry declares itself by form and content to be directly borrowed from the troubadours : it appeals to an aristocratic audience ; the idea of love as a feudal relation is preserved with the accompanying ideas of *amour courtois*, and the lyric forms developed in Southern France are imitated. The Provençal manner took root in Portugal as it failed to do in Spain, because it found the ground to some extent prepared by the existence of a popular lyric poetry which was remodelled under Provençal influence. The most popular of the types thus developed were *Cantigas de amor e de amigo* and *Cantigas de escarnho e de maldizer* ; the former were love songs : when the poet speaks the song was one *de amor* ; when the lady speaks (and she is unmarried, in contrast to Provençal usage) the song was *de amigo*. This latter is a type developed independently by the Portuguese school. *Cantigas de escarnho* correspond in intention to the Provençal *sirventes* ; if their satire was open and unrestrained they were *cantigas de maldizer*. They dealt for the most part with trivial court and personal affairs and not with questions of national policy upon which the troubadours so often expressed their opinions. Changes in taste and political upheavals brought this literature to an end about 1385 and the progress of Portuguese poetry then ceases for some fifty years.

CHAPTER IX

PROVENÇAL influence in Germany is apparent in
the lyric poetry of the minnesingers. Of these,
two schools existed, connected geographically with
two great rivers. The earlier, the Austro-Bavarian
school, flourished in the valley of the Danube :
the later minnesingers form the Rhine school. In
the latter case, Provençal influence is not disputed ;
but the question whether the Austro-Bavarian
school was exempt from it, has given rise to considerable discussion. The truth seems to be, that
the earliest existing texts representing this school
do show traces of Provençal influence ; but there
was certainly a primitive native poetry in these
Danube districts which had reached an advanced
stage of development before Provençal influence
affected it. Austria undoubtedly came into touch
with this influence at an early date. The Danube
valley was a high road for the armies of crusaders ;
another route led from Northern Italy to Vienna,
by which Peire Vidal probably found his way to
Hungary. At the same time, though Provençal

127

influence was strong, the Middle High German lyric rarely relapsed into mere imitation or translation of troubadour productions. Dietmar von Aist, one of the earliest minnesingers, who flourished in the latter half of the twelfth century has, for instance, the Provençal *alba* theme. Two lovers part at daybreak, when awakened by a bird on the linden : if the theme is Provençal, the simplicity of the poet's treatment is extremely fresh and natural. This difference is further apparent in the attitude of minnesingers and troubadours towards the conception of " love." The minnesong is the literary expression of the social convention known as " Frauendienst," the term " minne " connoting the code which prescribed the nature of the relation existing between the lover and his lady ; the dominant principle was a reverence for womanhood as such, and in this respect the German minnesang is inspired by a less selfish spirit than the Provençal troubadour poetry. Typical of the difference is Walter von der Vogelweide's—

> Swer guotes wîbes minne hât,
> der schamt sich aller missetât.

(" He who has a good woman's love is ashamed of every ill deed "), compared with Bernart de Ventadour's—

Non es meravilha s'ieu chan
Melhs de nul autre chantador
Car plus trai mos cors ves Amor
E melhs sui faitz a son coman.

(" It is no wonder if I sing better than any other
singer, for my heart draws nearer to love and I am
better made for love's command.")   The troubadour *amor*, especially in its Italian development,
eventually attained the moral power of the *minne* ;
but in its early stages, it was a personal and selfish
influence.   The stanza form and rime distribution
of the minnesinger poems continually betray Provençal influence :   the principle of tripartition is
constantly followed and the arrangement of rimes
is often a repetition of that adopted in troubadour
stanzas.   Friedrich von Hausen, the Count Rudolf
von Fenis, Heinrich von Morungen and others
sometimes translate almost literally from troubadour
poetry, though these imitations do not justify the
lines of Uhland,

In den Thälern der Provence ist der Minnesang entsprossen,
Kind des Frühlings und der Minne, holder, inniger Genossen.

Northern France, the home of epic poetry, also
possessed an indigenous lyric poetry, including
spring and dance songs, pastorals, romances, and
" chansons de toile." Provençal influence here
was inevitable. It is apparent in the form and

content of poems, in the attempt to remodel Provençal poems by altering the words to French forms, and by the fact that Provençal poems are found in MS. collections of French lyrics. Provençal poetry first became known in Northern France from the East, by means of the crusaders and not, as might be expected, by intercommunication in the centre of the country. The centre of Provençal influence in Northern France seems to have been the court of Eleanor of Poitiers the wife of Henry II. of England and the court of her daughter, Marie of Champagne. Here knights and ladies attempted to form a legal code governing love affairs, of which a Latin edition exists in the *De arte honeste amandi* of André le Chapelain, written at the outset of the thirteenth century. Well-known troubadours such as Bertran de Born and Bernart de Ventadour visited Eleanor's court and the theory of courtly love found its way into epic poetry in the hands of Chrétien de Troyes.

The Provençal school in Northern France began during the latter half of the twelfth century. The *chanson* properly so called is naturally most strongly represented : but the Provençal forms, the *tençon* (Prov. *tenso*) and a variant of it, the *jeu-parti* (Prov. *jocs partitz* or *partimens*) are also found, especially the latter. This was so called, because the opener of the debate proposed two alternatives to his

interlocutor, of which the latter could choose for
support either that he preferred, the proposer
taking the other contrary proposition : the con-
testants often left the decision in an *envoi* to one
or more arbitrators by common consent. Mis-
interpretation of the language of these *envois* gave
rise to the legend concerning the " courts of love,"
as we have stated in a previous chapter. One of
the earliest representatives of this school was
Conon de Bethune, born in 1155 ; he took part in
the Crusades of 1189 and 1199. Blondel de Nesles,
Gace Brulé and the Châtelain de Coucy are also
well-known names belonging to the twelfth century.
Thibaut IV., Count of Champagne and King of
Navarre (1201-1253), shared in the Albigeois crusade
and thus helped in the destruction of the poetry
which he imitated. One of the poems attributed
to him by Dante (*De Vulg. El.*) belongs to Gace
Brulé ; his love affair with Blanche of Castile is
probably legendary. Several crusade songs are
attributed to Thibaut among some thirty poems of
the kind that remain to us from the output of this
school. These crusade poems exhibit the characteristics of their Provençal models : there are exhortations to take the cross in the form of versified
sermons ; there are also love poems which depict
the poet's mind divided between his duty as a
crusader and his reluctance to leave his lady ;

or we find the lady bewailing her lover's departure,
or again, lady and lover lament their approaching
separation in alternate stanzas. There is more
real feeling in some of these poems than is apparent
in the ordinary chanson of the Northern French
courtly school : the following stanzas are from a
poem by Guiot de Dijon,[34] the lament of a lady for
her absent lover—

> Chanterai por mon corage
> Que je vueill reconforter
> Car avec mon grant damage
> Ne quier morir n'afoler,
> Quant de la terre sauvage
> Ne voi nului retorner
> Ou cil est qui m'assoage
> Le cuer, quant j'en oi parler
>   Dex, quant crieront outree,
>   Sire, aidiés au pelerin
>   Por cui sui espoentee,
>   Car felon sunt Sarrazin.
>
> De ce sui bone atente
> Que je son homage pris,
> E quant la douce ore vente
> Qui vient de cel douz païs
> Ou cil est qui m'atalente,
> Volontiers i tor mon vis :
> Adont m'est vis que jel sente
> Par desoz mon mantel gris.
>   Dex, etc.

" I will sing for my heart which I will comfort, for
in spite of my great loss I do not wish to die, and

yet I see no one return from the wild land where he
is who calms my heart when I hear mention of him.
God ! when they cry Outre (a pilgrim marching
cry), Lord help the pilgrim for whom I tremble, for
wicked are the Saracens.

"From this fact have I confidence, that I have
received his vows and when the gentle breeze blows
which comes from the sweet country where he is
whom I desire, readily do I turn my face thither :
then I think I feel him beneath my grey mantle."

The idea in the second stanza quoted is borrowed
from Bernard de Ventadour—

> Quant la douss' aura venta
> Deves vostre païs.
> Vejaire m'es qu'eu senta
> Un ven de Paradis.

The greater part of this poetry repeats, in another
language, the well-worn mannerisms of the troubadours : we find the usual introductory references
to the spring or winter seasons, the wounding glances
of ladies' eyes, the tyranny of love, the reluctance
to be released from his chains and so forth, decked
out with complications of stanza form and rime-
distribution. Dialectical subtlety is not absent,
and occasionally some glow of natural feeling may
be perceived ; but that school in general was careful
to avoid the vulgarity of unpremeditated emotion
and appealed only to a restricted class of the initiated.

Changes in the constitution and customs of society brought this school to an end at the close of the thirteenth century, and a new period of lyric poetry was introduced by Guillaume de Machaut and Eustache Deschamps.

Of the troubadours in England there is little to be said. The subject has hitherto received but scanty attention. Richard Cœur de Lion was as much French as English ; his mother, Queen Eleanor, as we have seen, was Southern French by birth and a patroness of troubadours. Richard followed her example ; his praises are repeated by many troubadours. What truth there may be in Roger of Hovenden's statement concerning his motives cannot be said ; " Hic ad augmentum et famam sui nominis emendicata carmina et rhythmos adulatorios comparabat et de regno Francorum cantores et joculatores muneribus allexerat ut de illo canerent in plateis, et jam dicebatur ubique, quod non erat talis in orbe." The manuscripts have preserved two poems attributed to him, one referring to a difference with the Dauphin of Auvergne, Robert I. (1169-1234), the other a lament describing his feelings during his imprisonment in Germany (1192-1194). Both are in French though a Provençal verson is extant of the latter. The story of Richard's discovery by Blondel is pure fiction.[35]

From the time of Henry II. to that of Edward I.
England was in constant communication with
Central and Southern France and a considerable
number of Provençals visited England at different
times and especially in the reign of Henry III. ;
Bernard de Ventadour, Marcabrun and Savaric
de Mauleon are mentioned among them. Though
opportunity was thus provided for the entry of
Provençal influence during the period when a
general stimulus was given to lyric poetry throughout Western Europe, Norman French was the
literary language of England during the earlier
part of that age and it was not until the second
half of the thirteenth century that English lyric
poetry appeared. Nevertheless, traces of Provençal
influence are unmistakably apparent in this Middle
English lyric poetry. But even before this time
Anglo-Latin and Anglo-Norman literature was
similarly affected. William of Malmesbury says
that the Norman Thomas, Archbishop of York,
the opponent of Anselm wrote religious songs in
imitation of those performed by jongleurs ; " si
quis in auditu ejus arte joculatoria aliquid vocale
sonaret, statim illud in divinas laudes effigiabat."
These were possibly hymns to the Virgin. There
remain also political poems written against John
and Henry III. which may be fairly called *sirventes*.
Latin disputes, such as those Inter Aquam et

Vinum, Inter Cor et Oculum, De Phillide et Flora, are constructed upon the principles of the *tenso* or *partimen*. The use of equivocal and " derivative " rimes as they are called in the Leys d'Amors is seen in the following Anglo-Norman stanzas. A poem with similar rimes and grouped in the same order is attributed to the Countess of Die, the Provençal *trobairitz* ; but this, as M. Paul Meyer points out, may be pure coincidence.[36]

> En lo sesoun qe l'erbe poynt
> E reverdist la matinée
> E sil oysel chauntent a poynt
> En temps d'avril en la ramée,
> Lores est ma dolur dublée
> Que jeo sui en si dure poynt
> Que jeo n'en ai de joie poynt,
> Tant me greve la destinée.
>
> Murnes et pensif m'en depart,
> Que trop me greve la partie ;
> Si n'en puis aler cele part,
> Que ele n'eyt a sa partie
> Mon quor tot enter saunz partie.
> E puis qu'el ad le men saunz part,
> E jeo n'oy unkes del soen part
> A moi est dure la partie.

" In the season when the grass springs and the morn is green and the birds sing exultantly in April time in the branches, then is my grief doubled, for I am in so hard a case that I have no joy at all, so heavy is my fate upon me.

" Sad and thoughtful I depart, for the case is too grievous for me : yet I cannot go thither, for she has in her power my heart whole and undivided. And since she has mine undivided and I never have any part of hers, the division is a hard one to me."

This influence was continued in Middle English lyric poetry. These lyrics are often lacking in polish ; the tendency to use alliteration as an ornament has nothing to do with such occasional troubadour examples of the trick as may be found in Peire d'Auvergne. Sometimes a refrain of distinctly popular origin is added to a stanza of courtly and artificial character. Generally, however, there is a freshness and vigour in these poems which may be vainly sought in the products of continental decadence. But Provençal influence, whether exerted directly or indirectly through the Northern French lyric school, is plainly visible in many cases. Of the lyrics found in the important MS. Harleian 2253,[37] " Alysoun " has the same rime scheme as a poem by Gaucelm Faidit : it opens with the conventional appeal to spring ; the poet's feelings deprive him of sleep. The Fair Maid of Ribbesdale has a rime-scheme almost identical with that shown by one of Raimbaut d'Aurenga's poems ; the description of the lady's beauty recalls many troubadour formulæ : the concluding lines—

He myhte sayen þat crist hym seze,
þat myhte nyhtes neh hyre leze,
heuene he hevede here.

are a troubadour commonplace. Many other
cases might be quoted. Hymns and songs to the
Virgin exhibit the same characteristics of form.
The few Provençal words which became English
are interesting; [38] colander or cullender (now a
vegetable strainer ; Prov. colador), funnel, puncheon,
rack, spigot, league, noose are directly derived from
Provençal and not through Northern French and
are words connected with shipping and the wine
trade, the port for which was Bordeaux.

.   .   .   .   .   .

In the year 1323 a society was formed in Toulouse
of seven troubadours, the " sobregaya companhia,"
for the purpose of preserving and encouraging lyric
poetry (lo gay saber). The middle class of Toulouse
seems at all times to have felt an interest in poetry
and had already produced such well-known troubadours as Aimeric de Pegulhan, Peire Vidal and
Guillem Figueira. The society offered an annual
prize of a golden violet for the best *chanso* ; other
prizes were added at a later date for the best dance
song and the best *sirventes*. Competitors found
that songs to the Virgin were given the preference
and she eventually became the one subject of these

prize competitions. The society produced a grammatical work, the Leys d'Amors, under the name of its president, Guillem Molinier, in 1356,[39] no doubt for the reference and instruction of intending competitors. The competition produced a few admirable poems, but anxiety to preserve the old troubadour style resulted generally in dry and stilted compositions. The *Academie des jeux floraux* [40] altered the character of the competition by admitting French poems after 1694. At the end of the sixteenth century, Provençal poetry underwent a revival ; in our own time, poets such as Jasmin, Aubanel, Roumanille and above all, Mistral, have raised their language from a patois to a literary power. The work of the félibres has been to synthetise the best elements of the various local dialects and to create a literary language by a process not wholly dissimilar to that described at the outset of this book. But the old troubadour spirit had died long before ; it had accomplished its share in the history of European literature and had given an impulse to the development of lyric poetry, the effects of which are perceptible even at the present day.

BIBLIOGRAPHY AND NOTES

LITERARY HISTORY

F. Diez, *Leben und Werke der Troubadours*, 2nd edit., re-edited by K. Bartsch, Leipsic, 1882. *Die Poesie der Troubadours*, 2nd edit., re-edited by K. Bartsch, Leipsic, 1883.

K. Bartsch, *Grundriss zur Geschichte der provenzalischen Literatur*, Elberfeld, 1872. A new edition of this indispensable work is in preparation by Prof. A. Pillet of Breslau. The first part of the book contains a sketch of Provençal literature, and a list of manuscripts. The second part gives a list of the troubadours in alphabetical order, with the lyric poems attributed to each troubadour. The first line of each poem is quoted and followed by a list of the MSS. in which it is found. Modern editors have generally agreed to follow these lists in referring to troubadour lyrics : *e.g.* B. Gr., 202, 4 refers to the fourth lyric (in alphabetical order) of Guillem Ademar, who is no. 202 in Bartsch's list.

A list of corrections to this list is given by Gröber in Böhmer's *Romanische Studien*, vol. ii. 1875-77, Strassburg. In vol. ix. of the same is Gröbers' study of troubadour MSS. and the relations between them.

A. Stimming, *Provenzalische Literatur* in Gröber's *Grundriss der Romanischen Philologie*, Strassburg, 1888, vol. ii. part ii. contains useful bibliographical notices.

A. Restori, *Letteratura provenzale*, Milan, 1891 (*Manuali Hoepli*), an excellent little work.

A. Jeanroy, *Les origines de la poésie lyrique en France*, 2nd edit., Paris, 1904.

J. Anglade, *Les troubadours*, Paris, 1908, an excellent and trustworthy work, in popular style, with a good bibliography.

J. H. Smith, *The troubadours at Home*, 2 vols., New York, 1899 ;

popularises scientific knowledge by impressions of travel in Southern France, photographs, and historical imagination : generally stimulating and suggestive. Most histories of French literature devote some space to Provençal ; *e.g.* Suchier & Birch-Hirschfeld, *Geschichte der französischen Litteratur*, Leipsic, 1900. The works of Millot and Fauriel are now somewhat antiquated. *Trobador Poets*, Barbara Smythe, London, 1911, contains an introduction and translations from various troubadours.

DICTIONARIES AND GRAMMARS

F. Raynouard, *Lexique roman*, 6 vols., Paris, 1838-1844, supplemented by

E. Levy, *Provenzalisches supplement-Wörterbuch*, Leipsic, 1894, not yet completed, but indispensable.

E. Levy, *Petit dictionnaire provençal-français*, Heidelberg, 1908.

J. B. Roquefort, *Glossaire de la langue romane*, 3 vols., Paris, 1820.

W. Meyer-Lübke, *Grammaire des langues romanes*, French translation of the German, Paris, 1905.

C. H. Grandgent, *An outline of the phonology and morphology of old Provençal*, Boston, 1905.

H. Suchier, *Die französiche und provenzalische Sprache* in Gröber's *Grundriss*. A French translation, *Le Français et le Provençal*, Paris, 1891.

TEXTS

The following chrestomathies contain tables of grammatical forms (except in the case of Bartsch) texts and vocabularies.

Altprovenzalisches Elementarbuch, O. Schultz-Gora, Heidelberg, 1906, an excellent work for beginners.

Provenzalische Chrestomathie, C. Appel, Leipsic, 1907, 3rd edit.

Manualetto provenzale, V. Crescini, Padua, 1905, 2nd edit.

Chrestomathie provençal, K. Bartsch, re-edited by Koschwitz, Marburg, 1904.

The following editions of individual troubadours have been published.

Alegret. *Annales du Midi*, no. 74.

Arnaut Daniel. U. A. Canello, Halle, 1883.

Bernart de Rovenac. G. Borsdorff, Erlangen, 1907.

Bartolomeo Zorzi. E. Levy, Halle, 1883.

Bertran d'Alamanon. J. Salverda de Grave, Toulouse, 1902 (*Bibliothèque Méridionale*).

Bertran de Born. A. Thomas, Toulouse, 1888 (*Bibliothèque Méridionale*).

Bertran de Born. A. Stimming, Halle, 1892 (and in the *Romanische Bibliothek*, Leipsic).

Blacatz. O. Soltau, Leipsic, 1890.

Cercamon. Dr Dejeanne, Toulouse, 1905 (*Annales du Midi*, vol. xvii.).

Elias de Barjols. Stronski, Paris, 1906 (*Bibliothèque Méridionale* vi.).

Folquet de Marselha. Stronski, Cracow, 1911.

Folquet de Romans. Zenker (*Romanische Bibliothek*).

Gavaudan. A. Jeanroy, *Romania*, xxxiv., p. 497.

Guillaume IX. Comte de Poitiers. A. Jeanroy, Toulouse, 1905.

Guillem Anelier de Toulouse. M. Gisi, Solothurn, 1877.

Guillem de Cabestanh. F. Hüffer, Berlin, 1869.

Guillem Figueira. E. Levy, Berlin, 1880.

Guillem de Montanhagol. J. Coulet, *Bibliothèque Méridionale*, iv., Toulouse.

Guiraut de Bornelh. A. Kolsen, Berlin, 1894 and 1911.

Guiraut d'Espanha. P. Savi-Lopez. *Studj mediœvali*, Fasc. 3, Turin, 1905.

Guiraut Riquier, Étude sur, etc. J. Anglade, Paris, 1905.

Jaufre Rudel. A Stimming, Kiel, 1873.

Marcabrun. Dr Dejeanne. *Bibliothèque Méridionale*, 1910.

Marcoat. Dr Dejeanne, Toulouse, 1903 (*Annales du Midi*, xv.).

Monk of Montaudon. E. Philippson, Halle, 1873 ; O. Klein, Marburg, 1885.

N' At de Mons. Bernhard. *Altfranzösische Bibliothek, Heilbronn*.

Paulet de Marselha. E. Levy, Paris, 1882.

Peire d'Alvernhe (d'Auvergne). R. Zenker, Rostock, 1900.

Peire Vidal. K. Bartsch, Berlin, 1857 (an edition by J. Anglade is about to appear).

Peire Rogier. C. Appel, Berlin, 1892.

Perdigon. H. J. Chaytor, *Annales du Midi*, xxi.

Pons de Capdoill. M. Napolski, Halle, 1879.

Raimbaut de Vaqueiras. O. Schultz, Halle, 1893.

Raimon de Miraval, Étude sur, etc. P. Andraud, Paris, 1902.

Sordel. De Lollis, Halle, 1896 (*Romanische Bibliothek*).

Numerous separate pieces have been published in the various periodicals concerned with Romance philology, as also have diplomatic copies of several MSS. Of these periodicals, the most important for Provençal are *Romania, les Annales du Midi, Zeitschrift der Romanischen Philologie, Archiv für das Studium der neueren Sprachen, Romanische Studien, Studj di filologia romanza, Revue des langues romanes*. Mahn's *Gedichte der Troubadours*, 4 vols., Berlin, 1856-71, contains diplomatic copies of MSS. ; his *Werke der Troubadours*, Berlin, 1846-55, contains reprints from Raynouard, *Choix des poésies originales des Troubadours*, Paris, 1816. Suchier, *Denkmäler provenzalischer Sprache*, Halle, 1883 ; Appel, *Provenzalische Inedita*, Leipsic, 1890 ; Chabaneau, *Poesies inédites des Troubadours du Périgord*, Paris, 1885 ; P. Meyer, *Les derniers troubadours de Provence*, Paris, 1871, should be mentioned. Most of the pieces in the *Parnasse Occitanien*, Toulouse, 1819, are to be found better edited elsewhere. Other pieces are to be found in various *Festschriften* and occasional or private publications, too numerous to be detailed here. C. Chabaneau, *Les biographies des Troubadours*, Toulouse, 1885 (part of the *Histoire générale de Languedoc*) is full of valuable information. The biographies have been translated by I. Farnell, *Lives of the Troubadours*, London, 1896.

CHAPTER I

1. See maps at the end of Gröber's *Grundriss*, vol. i.

2. *De Vulg. El.* I., 8 : alii oc, alii oïl, alii si affirmando loquuntur, and *Vita Nuova*, xxv. Dante also knew the term provincialis.

3. Boethius. F. Hündgen, Oppeln, 1884. For Sainte Foy d'Agen, see *Romania* xxxi., p. 177 *ff*.

4. P. Meyer in *Romania* v., p. 257. Bédier, *Les chansons de Croisade*, Paris, 1909, p. 16.

5. See P. Maus, *Peire Cardenals Strophenbau*, Marburg, 1884.
6. See Jeanroy, Origines, etc.

CHAPTER II

7. Provençal has also the feminine *joia* with the general meaning of " delight."
8. See Stimming's article in Gröber's *Grundriss*.
9. Raynouard, *Les Troubadours et les Cours d'Amour*, Paris, 1817 ; see also Diez, *Über die Minnehöfe*, Berlin, 1825. Pio Rajna, *Le Corti d'Amore*, Milan, 1890.
10. *Annales du Midi*, xix. p. 364.
11. *Die provenzalische Tenzone*, R. Zenker, Leipsic, 1888.

CHAPTER III

12. Girart de Roussillon, translation by P. Meyer, Paris, 1884 : see also *Romania*, vii. Diplomatic copies of the MSS. in *Romanische Studien* V. *Le Roman de Flamenca*, P. Meyer, Paris, 1901.
13. J. B. Beck, *Die Melodien der Troubadours*, Strasburg, 1908. *La Musique des Troubadours*, Paris, 1910, by the same author, who there promised a selection of songs harmonized for performance : this has not yet appeared. See also *Quatre poésies de Marcabrun*, Jeanroy, Dejeanne and Aubry, Paris, 1904, with texts, music, and translations.
14. Schindler, *Die Kreuzzüge in der altprovenzalischen und mittel-hochdeutschen lyrik.*, Dresden, 1889. K. Lewent, *Das altprovenzalische Kreuzlied*, Berlin, 1905.
15. A. Pillet, *Studien zur Pastourelle*, Breslau, 1902. Römer, *Die volkstümlichen Dichtungsarten der altprovenzalischen Lyrik*, Marburg, 1884.
16. *Quae judicia de litteris fecerint Provinciales*, P. Andraud, Paris, 1902.
17. From *Si·m sentis fizels amics*, quoted by Dante, *De Vulg. El.* i. 9.

K

Chapter IV

18. " Paubre motz " ; also interpreted as " scanty words," *i.e.*
poems with short lines. On Jaufre Rudel in literature, see a
lecture by Carducci, Bologna 1888. The latest theory of his
mysterious love is that she was the Virgin Mary ; see C. Appel,
Archiv für das Studium der neueren Sprachen, cvii. 3-4.

19. Mahn, *Gedichte*, no. 707. An edition of Bernard de Ventadour's poems is in preparation by Prof. Appel.

20. *Cp.* Dante, *Par.* xx. 73.

Chapter V

21. Dante, *De Vulg. El.* ii. 2.

22. " Il Provenzale," *Conv.* iv. 11.

23. *Purg.* xxvi.

24. On his family see Stronski, *Folquet de Marseille*, p. 15 and 159-
172.

25. See G. Paris, *La Littérature française au moyen âge*, § 128.

Chapter VI

26. The best short account of the Albigenses is to be found in vol. i.
of H. C. Lea's *Histoire de L'Inquisition au moyen âge*, Paris,
1903. This, the French translation, is superior to the English
edition as it contains the author's last corrections, and a
number of bibliographical notes. The Adoptionist theory
is stated in the introduction to F. C. Conybeare's *Key of
Truth*, Oxford, 1908. The *Chanson de la Croisade Albigeoise*,
P. Meyer, Paris, 1875, 2 vols., is indispensable to students of
the subject. In these works will be found much of the ex-
tensive bibliography of the heresy and crusade.

27. Eckbertus, *Serm. adv. Catharos*, *Migne, Patr. Lat.*, tom. 193,
p. 73.

28. *Cf.* Milman, *Latin Christianity*, Book IX. chap. viii. p. 85.

29. On religious lyric poetry, see Lowinsky, *Zeitschrift für franzö-
sische Sprache und Litteratur*, xx. p. 163 *ff.*, and the bibliographical note to Stimming's article in Gröber's *Grundriss*,
vol. ii. part ii. § 32.

CHAPTER VII

Most histories of Italian literature deal with this subject. See Gaspary's *Italian Literature to the death of Dante*: H. Oelsner, Bohn's Libraries. See also the chapter, *La poésie française en Italie* in Jeanroy's *Origines*. For Dante, see *Storia letteraria d'Italia, scritta di una società di professori*, Milan, vol. iii., Dante, by Zingarelli. *The Troubadours of Dante*, Chaytor, Oxford, 1902. Useful are A. Thomas, *Francesco da Barberino et la littérature provençale en Italie au moyen âge*, Paris, 1883. O. Schultz, *Die Lebensverhältnisse der Italienischen Trobadors*, Berlin, 1883.

30. Schultz, *Die Briefe des Trobadors Raimbaut de Vaqueiras an Bonifaz I.*, Halle, 1883.
31. Zingarelli, *Intorno a due Trovatori in Italia*, Florence, 1899.

CHAPTER VIII

Milà y Fontañals, *Los trovadores en España*, Barcelona, 1861, remains the best work on the subject. On Portugal, the article in Gröber's *Grundriss*, ii. 2, p. 129, by C. Michaelis de Vasconcellos and Th. Braga is admirable : see the bibliographical references there given and the introduction to R. Lang, *Das Liederbuch des Königs Denis von Portugal*, Halle, 1894.

32. The date of this poem is disputed, see Dr Dejeanne's edition of Marcabrun, p. 235.
33. F. Guessard, *Grammaires Provençales*, Paris, 1858 ; E. Stengel, *Die beiden ältesten prov. Gram.*, Marburg, 1878.

CHAPTER IX

Troubadour influence in Germany is discussed at greater or less length in most histories of German literature. See Jeanroy, *Origines*, p. 270 *ff*. A. Lüderitz, *Die Liebestheorien der Provenzalen bei den Minnesingern der Stauferzeit*, Literarhistorische Forschungen, Berlin, 1904.

For France. A. Jeanroy, *De nostratibus medii aevi poetis qui primum Aquitaniæ carmina imitati sint*, Paris, 1889.

For England. Schofield, *English Literature from the Norman Conquest to Chaucer*, London, 1906. O. Heider, *Untersuchungen zur mittelenglischen erotischen Lyrik*, Halle, 1905. A. Brandl, *Spielmann's verhältnisse in frühmittelenglischer Zeit*, Sitzungs-berichte der Königl. preuss., Akademie, 1910.

34. Bédier, *Chansons de Croisade*, Paris, 1909, p. 112.
35. See introduction to Leo Wiese, *Die Lieder des Blondel de Nesle*, Dresden, 1904, p. 19 *ff*.
36. *Romania*, viii. p. 370.
37. K. Böddeker, *Altenglische Dichtungen des MS. Harl.* 2253, Berlin, 1878.
38. Modern Language Review, vol. 1. p. 285 ; vol. ii. p. 60, articles by Prof. Skeat.
39. P. Leinig, *Grammatik der provenzalischen Leys d'amors verglichen mit der Sprache der Troubadours*, Breslau, 1890. M. Gatien. Arnoult, *Monuments de la littérature romane*, Toulouse, 1841.
40. *Histoire critique de l'Académie des Jeux Floraux*, by F. de Gélis from the origin to the 17th century will appear shortly in the Bibliothèque meridionale, Toulouse. Useful anthologies of modern Provençal are *Flourilège prouvençau*, Toulon, 1909 : *Antologia provenzale*, E Portal, Milan, Hoepli, 1911 (Manuali Hoepli).

INDEX

149